R. A. Whitehead

Austrian
Steam
Locomotives

An Introductory Survey 1837 to 1980

R. A. Whitehead
Tonbridge, Kent
1982

Published by R. A. Whitehead & Partners,
172a High Street,
Tonbridge, Kent TN9 1BE.

Front cover picture: Südbahn 4-4-0 No. 399 (Floridsdorf 1010/1896)
   standing at Kufstein with an express for Innsbruck

Cover design: Ken Wilson

Photographs: Sources of photographs are individually acknowledged.
   The author extends his sincerest thanks to each of them.

Typeset by Goodfellow & Egan Phototypesetting Ltd., Cambridge

Print Management and Consultancy: Impression Ltd, Willingham, Cambridge

Printed and bound by Pendragon Press, Papworth, Cambs

Map by M. Patrick

ISBN 0 9508298 03

Contents

Successive Official Titles of the State Railway undertaking in Austria

Since	Initials	Official title and translation
1.7.1884	kk. St. B	kaiserlich-konigliche österreichische Staatsbahnen (Imperial-royal Austrian State Railways)
12.11.1918	DÖ St. B	Deutsch österreichische Staatsbahnen (German-Austrian State Railways)
21.10.1919	Ö St. B	Österreichische Staatsbahnen (Austrian State Railways)
1.4.1921	BBÖ	Bundesbahnen Österreich (Federal Railways Austria)
18.3.1938	DRB	Deutsche Reichsbahn
27.4.1945	Ö St. B	Österreichische Staatseisenbahnen (Austrian State Railways)
5.8.1947	ÖBB	Österreichische Bundesbahnen

Other abbreviations employed

1) Railways

CSD	Ceskoslovenske stetni drahy (Czechoslavakian State Railways)
EWA	Eisenbahn Wien Aspang
GKB	Graz-Köflacher Bahn
HF	Heeresfeldbahn (German Military Field Railways)
KEB	Kaiserin Elizabeth Bahn
KFJB	Kaiser Franz Josef Bahn
KFNB	Kaiser Ferdinands Nordbahn
KRB	Kronprinz Rudolf Bahn
NÖLB	Niederösterreichische Landesbahnen (Lower Austrian Provincial Railways)
NÖSWB	Niederösterreichische Sudwestbahn
ÖNWB	Österreichische Nordwestbahn
SKGLB	Salzkammergut Lokalbahn
SULM	Sulmtalbahn
StEG	Österreichisch-ungarische Staatseisenbahngesellschaft

2) Locomotive Builders

Chrz	Pierwsza Fabryka Lokomotyo w Polsce S.A., Chrzanov, Poland

First Bohemian Erste Bohmisch – Marische Maschinfabrike, Prague.

Flor	Wiener Lokomotivfabrik AG., Floridsdorf, Wien, Austria.
Kr. Linz	Locomotivfabrik Krauss, Linz, Upper Austria.
Kr.Munich	Locomotivfabrik Krauss, Munich, Bavaria.
Sigl	G. Sigl Locomotivfabrik, Wiener Neustadt, Lower Austria.
St. EG	Maschin-Fabrik der Österreichisch – ungarische staats – eisenbahn Gesellschaft, Vienna.
WN	Actien-Gesellschaft der Lokomotivfabrik Wiener Neustadt, (formerly G. Sigl) Wiener Neustadt, Lower Austria.

Foreword
by Professor Doktor Adolph Giesl-Gieslingen

When author R. A. Whitehead introduced himself by sending me his 1978 book "Garrett 200" on the bicentenary history of the Garretts of Leiston, I was immediately impressed by his choice and treatment of a subject of rare interest, typical of the ups and downs of an enterprise started, developed and steered through the stormy and treacherous business world by men of great energy and vision. And, being likewise impressed by the clear and catching language, I felt and wrote to the author that his so extremely instructive book should indeed be made compulsory reading for students of business management!

Having thus had first-hand proof of Mr. R. A. Whitehead's ability to penetrate into, grasp and communicate to others the essentials of intricate subjects and complicated developments, I was delighted to learn that he was working on a book destined to acquaint the British reader with the history of the Austrian railways and their steam locomotives, seen also in the light of the European political scene, and of the Austrian in particular, from the days when railway traction began its victorious battle against all adversities.

Now that his book is presented to the interested public, it is my privilege and pleasure to state that, in my considered opinion, it admirably fills a real want inasmuch as, in spite of the close ties between British and Austrians, nothing had yet been produced to tell the story of the latters' railways in the English language, nor even in German when judging from the standpoint of completeness and political background.

Adolph Giesl-Gieslingen

Vienna, May 1982

Austrian Locomotives
Preface

I shall perhaps be thought presumptuous in attempting to write on the subject of Austrian locomotives. The urge to do so comes from the fact that a breed for which I have the greatest admiration has so few chroniclers in English so that, following G. K. Chesterton's dictum, "If a thing is worth doing it is worth doing badly," I have been emboldened to set my hand to it. We, my wife Jean and I, fell in love with Austria almost of first sight and repeated acquaintance has endeared the country and its people still further to us. This book is offered, with the greatest possible deference, as a trifling acknowledgement of the patience and kindness with which we have been received by the Austrians we have met, especially railwaymen.

We have travelled over almost all sections of Austrian railways having a passenger service and doing this has, naturally, brought us into contact with a great many railway people. No service on the scale of a national railway can be expected to be staffed entirely with paragons but the personnel of Ö.B.B. are able, we feel, to stand comparison with railwaymen anywhere, capable, usually cheerful, often humorous, tolerant of our comic German, and, most importantly, possessed of an intense pride in the railway service.

Though this book is based to some extent upon my own researches and observations it is necessarily mainly an anthology of the work of others. Indeed one of my hopes in writing it has been to provide an introduction to the impressive range of German language literature available to the student of Austrian locomotive practice.

The preface provides the forum and the welcome opportunity to acknowledge how much gratitude is owed to others for their encouragement and help. Foremost amongst these is Professor Doktor Adolph Giesl-Gieslingen, inventor, author and doyen of Austrian locomotive engineers, a witty and amusing companion and an unwearying collaborator who not only read and annotated the manuscript but also contributed the foreword. Tremendous encouragement has also been given by Herr Josef Otto and Frau Ilse Slezak who have arranged the use of most of the illustrations. Thanks are also due to the Directors and Staffs of the Austrian National Library and of the Vienna Technical Museum, the management of the Graz Koflacher Bahn at Graz and the helpful staff of the Steiermarkische Landesbahnen as well as an un-numbered host of anonymous Austrian railway personnel. Two British friends of long-standing who have interested themselves in the project and been very helpful are Bill Love and Derek Stoyel. They have read the manuscript, provided information and made comments which have been most useful. Help has also been given by Mr S. G. Morrison, Librarian of the Institution of Mechanical Engineers, Mr David Phillips of the Museum of English Rural Life, and my son-in-law Michael Walters. The photographers or owners of collections who have contributed illustrations are also thanked most heartily and photographs are ascribed individually to those who have provided them.

Published sources in English are not plentiful and the bulk of them are to be found in engineering journals, notably "The Engineer" and "Engineering", the specialised railway periodicals, "The Locomotive", "The Railway Magazine" and "The Railway Gazette", or in general or reference works. An account of the articulated locomotives entered in the Semmering Trials is contained, for instance, in Lionel Weiner's massive survey "Articulated Locomotives" but such references are, on the whole, scarce. Where reference has been made to recent publications, roughly those since 1960, preference has generally been given to

Austrian rather than English publications with the exception of Brian Reed's contributions to the Profile series on Norris locomotives, German Kriegsloks and Austrian 2-8-4s (jointly with Dr -Ing. Fr. Altmann).

The main current sources, however, have been the following German language books:

Lokomotivbau in Alt-Österreich – K. Gölsdorf
Die Ära nach Gölsdorf – A. Giesl-Gieslingen
Dampfbetrieb in Alt-Österreich – J. Stockklausner
Die Lokomotiven der Republik Österreich – J. O. Slezak
Schmalspurig durch Österreich – Krobot, Slezak and Sternhart
Krauss Lokomotiven – B. Schmeiser
Niederösterreichische Sudwestbahn – Sternhart and Slezak
Die Österreichische Nordwestbahn – A. Horn
Die Kaiser Ferdinands-Nordbahn – A. Horn

Those titles were all in print or about to be reprinted when this was written and it would be a source of satisfaction to me if, in a modest way, this book were to serve to increase their sales in England.

My wife Jean has joined in researches both in the field and in libraries, has read and annotated the manuscript, and checked proofs and the typing has been done by Mrs A. L. Inge who has endured with patience and cheerfulness many revisions of the draft.

Tonbridge, Kent.
July, 1982   R. A. Whitehead

Chapter I
The background of events

It is difficult to understand how Austrian locomotive history came to be what it was without knowing, in outline, the history and topography of the railway system the shapings of which in turn depended upon political events. To embark upon a political history of the country over the last 165 years would be entirely out of place here but the brief notes which follow, though a gross over-simplification of actual events, may be of some assistance.

Contemporary Austria is the predominantly German speaking rump of the former Austro-Hungarian empire, the combined domains fo which included not only the Kingdom of Hungary, but also what is now Czechoslavakia, parts of Rumania and Southern Poland, much of Yugoslavia and a considerable tract of Northern Italy.

Austria and its Hapsburg monarch, Franz I, (1768–1835) had the good fortune to emerge from the Napoleonic Wars on the winning side and largely by the exertions of Prince Metternich, the Austrian Chancellor, the disposing of European boundaries into what is was hoped, vainly as events turned out, would be stable and peaceable arrangements was undertaken at a congress of delegates at Vienna in 1815. With the exception of the representatives of Great Britain, Castlereagh and Canning, answerable to a Parliament elected on a very limited franchise, the delegates assembled represented absolute monarchs and the decisions taken reflected the real or supposed interests of the royal heads of state rather than national interests in the modern sense.

Metternich, the dominant figure of the congress and principal architect of the resultant treaty, an unswerving monarchist and a resolute enemy of all populist and nationalist aspirations, was oblivious to the wishes and, in general, the interests of the inhabitants of the territories the future government of which was settled at Vienna, his twin concerns being the maintenance or augmenting of the status and dominions of his royal masters and, so far as it was compatible with the first, the establishing of a balance of power in Europe. Britain, though interested in the prevention of a recurrence of a situation such as had arisen with the Napoleonic Empire, had no territorial ambitions in Europe but wished to curb, if possible, the power of Russia. In general, therefore, the British delegates alone could afford to take a moderately detached stance, the other parties being necessarily swayed by more direct interest in the outcome. The Treaty of Vienna was probably the last major territorial settlement in Europe reached by the processes of the old diplomacy without some reference to popular consent or aspirations.

For Austria the treaty, so carefully provided by Metternich with checks and balances, contained at least two major defects. Firstly Austria's expectation of playing a dominant role in the German speaking bloc placed it in direct opposition to Prussia which, having taken a large part in the defeat of Napoleon, now cast itself for the part of leader of the German confederation. Nothing in the treaty provided the means of reconciling these mutually antagonistic ambitions nor is it possible, given the respective attitudes of the parties, to see any way in which the problem might have been resolved other than by military conflict. This, in fact, was the way in which the question was ultimately decided though fifty-one years were to elapse before open war occurred. Secondly, by siting boundaries arbitrarily in contempt of linguistic or ethnic divisions and by reinforcing and buttressing absolute monarchies, the treaty actually created or promoted the growth of the democratic and nationalist reform groups it was intended to anathematise. A hundred years later manifestations of these same ethnic and linguistic antagonisms were to confound the efforts of those who drafted the Treaty of Versailles and its daughter treaties after the 1914/18 war.

During the fifteen years after the Congress of Vienna, in part by the efforts of Metternich, in part by the creation of a powerful and repressive secret police and a large and often heavy handed military presence, but in part also by the undoubted personal good qualities of the Emperor, which inspired affection in his subjects not entirely offset by his less desirable characteristics, to wit his notably narrow mindedness and stubborn opposition to change, the Empire was kept free of overt unrest. Indeed the only open disturbance in his lifetime was in 1830 in Lombardy where 30,000 Austrian troops were needed to keep order, though Austrian soldiers were used to suppress rebellions in neighbouring Parma and Modena and the Papal States. During this time he endeavoured, with the aid of his ministers, to prevent alterations in the national life-style, opposing innovation and supporting existing usages and institutions.

Because of his aversion to change only one railway line received the imperial assent in his lifetime – the horse worked Linz-Budweis line – designed to link the rivers Danube and Moldau and thus to make easier the portage in the otherwise water borne salt traffic between the mines of the Salzburg area and the industries of Bohemia.

His son, Ferdinand I, who succeeded him in 1835, has been characterised as "an amiable but weak-minded prince". He was, however, less total in his opposition to change and within weeks of his accession the Imperial assent was given to the proposed Nordbahn (Vienna to Cracow) the promoters of which had pressed their cause upon his father for five years without moving him. For the first ten years of his reign the mode of government remained much as in his father's time but repression was less efficient and the powers of insurgency were stronger. A rebellion in Galicia in 1846 was successfully put down but a revolt in Vienna itself in March 1848 secured some measures of reform and the flight of Metternich. An uprising in Lombardy and Venice, assisted by the King of Sardinia initially drove the Austrian forces out of Lombardy until it, in turn, was defeated in 1849 by General Radetzky. There was also revolt in Bohemia but in Hungary the bitter struggle of the Magyars for independence produced a state of civil war. Moreover the departure of the garrison of Vienna to serve in that war led to a revolt in the capital in sympathy with Hungary. The city was retaken by storm during 28th to 31st October, 1848, after an artillery bombardment, the burning of some of the suburbs and what was described as "a desperate struggle and an immense slaughter".

At the end of this year of struggle and carnage, on 2nd December, 1848 he abdicated and, his brother and legal successor, Franz Karl, having renounced the throne, the latter's son Franz Josef became emperor as Franz Josef I.

In the summer of 1849 the rebellion in Hungary was finally suppressed and in the sullen peace which enveloped the empire and kingdom, efforts were begun to right the time lag which the conservatism of the two preceding reigns had brought about in the economic development of the country. A programme of construction of railways and roads was commenced, feudalism was abolished and taxation was made less onerous but politically the reforms exacted by the Viennese in 1848 were eaten away by an intensification of military rule.

By the mid eighteen fifties the new emperor apparently felt sufficiently secure upon the throne to begin the long process of pacification and reconciliation which was to take up the remainder of his reign. Royal visits to Italy to this end in 1856 and to Hungary in 1857 were so coldly received, however, as to amount to snubs. Austrian rule in Lombardy had not long to run for in January 1859 the people of Lombardy launched into revolt and set in motion the chain of events which culminated in the defeat of the Austrians at Magenta by a combined French and Sardinian army and the ceding of Lombardy, except for certain strategic fortresses, to Sardinia, the first step in the unification of Italy.

Austria joined Prussia in 1863 in annexing Schleswig and Holstein from Denmark but fell out with her erstwhile ally over the division of the spoils so that in 1866 she came to "the Seven Days War" with Prussia which she lost – parting in the resultant settlement with the very fortresses preserved in the earlier peace over Lombardy, giving a substantial cash indemnity to Prussia and making final abdication from any claim to head the German confederacy – the latter, as noted earlier, the underlying cause of the Prussian antipathy toward Austria.

Thereafter save for the accession of Bosnia and Herzogovina to the protection of Austria after the Treaty of Berlin of 1878 the boundaries of the empire remained unchanged until the aftermath of the 1914–18 war. The remainder of the long reign of Franz Josef I was lived, however, in the shadow of the divisive forces of nationalism, never, after the events of 1848, wholly quiescent and often shrilly strident. The setting up of a Parliament (the Reichsrath) in 1860, elected on a limited franchise (but not more limited than the contemporary franchise in this country) gave nationalism a platform rather than formed a uniting force. In Hungary particularly the dominant Magyars pressed ceaselessly for autonomy or independence. An accommodation was reached with them in 1867 by which Hungary achieved a status in relation to Austria which was the approximate equivalent of that of the dominions of Canada and Australia to Great Britain, that is united to Austria by the person of Franz Josef, who was emperor of Austria and king of Hungary. For purposes of internal administration Hungary enjoyed all but total autonomy but empire and kingdom were combined for foreign affairs and defence by a common council of ministers.

No similar arrangements were made, however, for other races in the empire. Bohemia, Moravia and Slovakia (which today form Czechoslovakia) were predominantly Slav, the South Tirol had a substantial Italian minority whilst Galicia was largely Polish. Whereas the Magyars had gained themselves a Parliament of roughly equal status to that of the Reichsrath the other non-German speaking elements of the population achieved no such autonomy. Nevertheless, despite the political dissent, the Empire was set on a course of real financial and industrial growth, of municipal reform, urban reconstruction and a limited but growing degree of representative government. The lack of a common language, however, defeated the objective of creating a general consensus of Austrian citizenship. Constitutional concessions to the Czechs were used by them against their German speaking neighbours and those to the Slavs against their Italian compatriots. Notwithstanding these antipathies between linguistic groups and their repercussions in the Reichsrath the second half of the last century saw a great increase in industrial output, the breaking down of traditional restraints, symbolised perhaps by the dismantling (1858–60) of the fortifications enclosing the old city of Vienna and the construction of the magnificently conceived Ring on the site of them; and the initiation of social reforms – regulation of factories and mines, sewering of towns and cities and provision of much improved drinking water supplies to major towns. Water for Vienna is brought to the city from underground reservoirs to the South West through a vast pipeline commenced in the seventies.

By the end of the century the rate of economic growth had slowed and money had become scarcer but by that time most of the great railways and many of the branches had been accomplished. The last major line constructed by the old empire and kingdom was the line South from Klagenfurt to Feistritz in Rosental and on southwards via the Karawanken Tunnel but there was still activity in the construction of local railways, many of 760cm gauge. The period of reform and progress in public affairs in the last three decades of the nineteenth century had been paralleled by a series of anarchist outrages in the eighties and by bitter Parliamentary strife through most of the thirty years. Royal affairs, full of hope in the seventies, went through a series of misfortunes and tragedies borne by the Emperor with stoicism and dignity. His eldest son and heir to the throne Rudolf, who had entered into a morganatic marriage with a commoner, committed suicide at Mayerling in 1889. Seven years later the Empress Elizabeth was assassinated by a Bavarian extremist and in 1914 the Emperor's nephew and heir, Franz Ferdinand, and his wife Sophie were shot dead by a Slav extremist at Sarajevo in the incident which precipitated the 1914/18 war.

Franz Josef I died in 1916. His great nephew Karl who followed him to the throne reigned only two years. The empire and kingdom had already been under considerable internal stresses from mutual antagonism amongst its racial groups before the war began and under the further terrible stresses imposed by the war and the death of Franz Josef progressive disintegration set in. From the defeat of the Central Powers in 1918 Austria emerged like a sheep from the shearers, stripped to the lean and shivering shape of the eight Landes of Vorarlberg, Tyrol, Salzburgland, Upper and Lower Austria, Steiermark, Styria and Carinthia to be joined, after a plebiscite in 1921, by part of the former Hungarian province of Burgehland as a ninth Land. Hungary and Czechoslovakia (Bohemia, Moravia and Slovakia) achieved total independence, South Tyrol was joined to Italy, Transylvania to Rumania, Galicia to the newly independent Poland, whilst Croatia, Slovenia, Dalmatia, Boznia and Hertzogovina became part of the new state of Yugoslavia.

The new Republic of Austria had thus to overcome the loss of the greater part of its industry, most of its coal and almost all of its wealth. The triumphs of the post war years were great progress in working class housing in Vienna, electrification of the railways to use home produced electricity, the development of tourism and the institution of a new currency, of which the schilling was the basic unit, to replace the old currency debased by inflation. The reverse of the coin was great economic difficulties, a bitter conflict between left and right in politics, sporadic rioting in Vienna with conflict between Socialists and Communists on one hand and Fascists and the rising Nazi party on the other, and a series of political assassinations, culminating in 1934 in near civil war after the assassination of the Conservative chancellor Dr Dolfuss.

Dolfuss was succeeded as Chancellor by Schuschnigg who endeavoured to offset the rising power of the Nazis by appealing to the Fascists. The suggestion of union with Germany as a way out of the economic and political distresses was canvassed with vigour and in 1938 Schuschnigg proposed, or at least acquiesced in, the holding, on 13th March, of a national plebiscite to decide for or against such union. Hitler preempted the issue by marching into Austria on 11th March, two days before the plebiscite was to be held. Not only was Austria soon to be disillusioned by the crudities and brutality of the Nazi regime but it was also to be dragged with Germany into the Second World War.

For the second time in a generation she emerged shattered from a conflict in which the majority of her people had not been willing participants, this time to face occupation (until

1956) by the victorious powers, Russia in Burgenland, Lower Austria and part of Upper Austria, the Americans in the rest of Upper Austria and Salzburg, the French in the Tyrol and Vorarlberg and the British in Styria and Carinthia. With the help of the Marshall Plan from 1945 to 1962 coupled with prodigious native effort the Austrians rebuilt and enhanced the country and its commerce in an Austrian parallel of the German 'Economic Miracle".

How these successive events shaped the railway system of Austria as it now is we shall explore in the following pages.

Chapter II
An outline of the system's history

Despite the fact that mining in Austria made early and consistent use of wooden railways – from the first half of the fifteenth century, if not even earlier – these were virtually confined to underground haulage and remained without influence on the general adoption of railways. The late Dr Lewis reported records of underground haulage in the mines at Schladming in the Salzkammergut as early as 1408. Other early uses were in the great silver and copper mine of Falkenstein at Schwaz, on the River Inn below Innsbruck (first recorded in 1564), at Kitzbühel (1614) and in the iron ore mines at Eisenerz (1655). All were narrow gauge using small wooden wagons propelled by one man. The salt mines of the Salzburg area had underground railways at Salzburg itself by 1616 and at the Durrenberg mines in 1720. The author travelled on the electrically operated successor of the Durrenberg lines in 1979. Whilst these underground railways which, as a type, had long lives had no part in the promotion of later surface railways there was a minor and indirect connection in that the line which is usually looked upon as the parent of Austrian railways – the horse worked line from Budweis to Linz – arose from the salt traffic from the mines of the Salzkammergut to Bohemia.

Salt had been carried for centuries down the River Salzach to the Danube and thence to Linz from which it was carried overland to Budweis (Ceske-Budejovice) on the River Moldau from which, again, it could be water borne. The portage had a hampering effect on an otherwise expanding trade and in 1808 A. Ritter von Gerstner, Professor of Mathematics at the University of Prague who was aware of mineral railway development in the North of England proposed that a similar railway should be made to link the Danube and the Moldau. Gerstner's proposed termini were Linz on the Danube and Joachimsmuhle on the Moldau but the line in this form never reached fruition, the country being involved in the terminal years of the long-running struggle to defeat Napoleon. It was not, in fact, until 1824, nine years after the Congress of Vienna that an amended project for a wood and iron railway, promoted by Gerstner's son, to run between Mauthausen and Budweis on the Danube and Moldau respectively, received Royal sanction.

Gerstner the younger became a convert to locomotive haulage from his acquaintance with the steam operated colliery railways of Northumbria during a visit to England in 1820 but, in fact, had to content himself with animal traction for his line. The railway, to the unusual gauge of 1106mm, was built with difficulty and was opened section by section as completed, the first on September 7th, 1827 and the final section on August 1st, 1832. During construction further sanction was obtained for the Danube terminus to be diverted from Mauthausen to Linz, increasing the length of the route to 128.8km on which from April 1st, 1833, passengers were carried. Two years later the railway was extended south-westward from Linz to Wels and finally, in 1836, to the town of Gmunden on the Traunsee, terminating in the Rathausplatz, terminus of the present Stern & Hafferl street electric tramway linking the town to the main-line station. The section Linz-Gmunden was converted to steam traction in 1854 but horse-drawn trains ran on the original line until 1872 when it was abandoned. From 1857 the line became part of the undertaking of the Kaiserin Elizabeth Railway (Vienna – Salzburg), discussed at greater length later in the Chapter, by whom it was converted to standard gauge.

The Linz-Budweiser Bahn was not only the first railway in Austria but was also probably the first narrow gauge public railway in Europe. Moreover, even in the days of horse-traction it was no mossy country branch. In 1836 the equipment included 59 passenger coaches, 762 goods wagons and of the order of eight hundred haulage horses. Despite the scale of its operation it suffered, however, from the fundamental draw-back that it had been conceived in the image of colliery railways and as an adjunct of industry rather than as a transport agency per se. It was soon to be followed by two railways cast in a more heroic mould.

Just as a period of five years in England from 1825 to 1830 – the age difference between the Stockton and Darlington and the Liverpool and Manchester – marked the essential change in the vision of a railway from that of an extended siding linking coal pits to their staithes, with passenger traffic a trifling incidental item, to that of the means of linking city to city and supplanting the stage coaches for the carriage of passengers and mails, so in Austria the nine years between 1827 and 1836 saw the contrast between the beginning of the construction of the Linz-Budweiser – to carry salt between two rivers – and the authorising of the Northern Railway, a concern with a mainline 413km long stretching from Vienna through Moravia and Galicia to Cracow (now in Poland) linking the coal and salt mines of Galicia with Vienna and Bohemia. The vision of Professor Franz Xavier Riepl of the Vienna Polytechnic Institute in 1829, the Northern Railway was paired in his design with a balancing arm south from Vienna over the Alps into Styria and Carinthia and on to the Adriatic port of Triest. Though the total opposition to change led by the Emperor Franz I inhibited further railway building in Austria, Riepl was fortunate in securing the backing of the Viennese banker, Soloman von Rothschild for what must have seemed to many practical men to be mere pipe-dreams incapable of realisation. As Rothschild's emissary he visited England in January 1830 to study and report upon the Liverpool and Manchester and other railways then in building, and to see locomotives on that railway and elsewhere. Making the acquaintance of Robert Stephenson convinced him that the future lay with locomotive traction, a conviction in which he succeeded in carrying his backer with him. Politically the time was not right, however, for railway promotion and it was not until the accession of Ferdinand I in 1835 that a consortium headed by Rothschild received a royal charter and royal backing for the construction of the Kaiser Ferdinands Nordbahn (KFNB). The 13km from Deutsch-Wagram to Floridsdorf on the North East fringes of Vienna, were opened on 17th November, 1837 and into Vienna North Station on 6th January, 1838. By the summer of 1842 the line was complete to Leipnik (198km) but nearly five years were to elapse before the succeeding 78km stretch to Oderberg was opened enabling through running to take place to Cracow though the 40km form Trzebinia to Cracow had been open, in isolation, since 1847. For these delays the internal upheavals in the country, narrated in the introduction, were mainly responsible. Of this railway only the initial 80km from Vienna to the present Czech border remains Austrian, along with the line to Marchegg (opened 1848), part of the branch to Zellerndorf (opened 1873) and the short branch to Zistersdorf, completed under lokalbahn legislation in 1889.

The other financial syndicate interested in railway promotion in Austria in the late 1830's was that headed by Baron Sina, to whom in March 1838 was granted the privilege of building the Vienna-Raab (now Györ, in Hungary) Railway, opened as far as Bruck a.d. Leitha in 1841, together with a second line from Vienna via Wiener Neustadt to Neunkirchen from which it was extended the following year to Gloggnitz on the North approach to the Semmering Pass.

Southwards from Gloggnitz the way was barred by the terrifying obstacle of the Alps through which it was planned to take the railway by way of the Semmering Pass – a task the eventual successful completion of which, by the Government, occupied twelve years. Whilst the Semmering line was in building the lines south of the Alps were pushed ahead – from Murzzuschlag to Graz in October 1844 and on to the present border station with Yugoslavia (Spielfeld-Strass) twenty months later. This line, from Vienna to Gloggnitz, over the Semmering to Murzzuschlag and on to Marburg became the nucleus of the later Sudbahn company.

It is said that the decision to build the Semmering Railway was taken on the personal initiative of the new Emperor Franz Josef I to provide employment in the economic and social distress which followed the revolutions and the suppression in 1848. During the decade that followed government investment in railways was substantial but in the second half of the fifties a crippling shortage of money overtook the imperial administration which led to the sale of substantial mileages of railway, including the line over the Semmering and south westward to Triest, to private companies often at prices very much below the real value of the assets changing hands and certainly at very much less than the monies expended upon construction. Promotion of new railways for the next fifteen years became a matter largely for private speculation, suffering a temporary set-back by reason of the war with Prussia but rising to a crescendo in the opening years of the seventies, when what bordered on railway mania swept the country, ending in financial crisis and much loss to the less wary investors. The money for the purchase of the Sudbahn was provided by the Credit Anstalt, in the affairs of which the Vienna and Paris branches of the Rothschild family and the English banker Samuel Laing were prominent.

Despite the set-back of 1866 and the final over-shadowing by financial crises that period (1858–1873) was vitally formative. A further Sudbahn line was begun leaving the original Vienna-Triest line at Marburg (now just inside Yugoslavia), heading westward along the River Drau to Klagenfurt (reached in June 1863), on to Villach (1864) and from thence North westward to Spittal, on through the East and South Tyrol (Italian since 1918) to Franzensfeste where it divided into two – South to Ala on the route to Verona and North, over the Brenner Pass, to Innsbruck (reached in late summer 1867). The completion in 1873 of a direct line Bruck a.d. Mur to Leoben (Sudbahn) and on to Villach (the Kronprinz Rudolf Bahn –KRB) shortened this route by following the hypotenuse of the Bruck, Marburg, Villach triangle.

It also became possible in the same period to reach Innsbruck from Vienna by the North route. The Kaiserin Elizabeth Bahn (Westbahn) from a new station in West Vienna to Salzburg and on to the Bavarian border (opened Vienna-Linz in December, 1858 and throughout the following August) linked with the Bavarian Railways West of Salzburg and by travelling through Bavaria via Rosenheim to Kufstein (on the Bavarian/Austrian border North East of Innsbruck) it was possible to join the railway from Kufstein to Innsbruck, on Austrian soil, opened in November, 1858 by the Sudbahn.

Heady plans were afoot in 1873 to join Innsbruck to the Vorarlberg and the West by a new line tunnelling under the formidable obstacle of the Arlberg but it fell a casualty to the crisis at the end of the year, though the direct link line from Salzburg to Wörgl (on the existing line from Kufstein to Innsbruck), the first section of which, from Salzburg to Hallein, was opened in 1871, was eventually completed and was opened in August 1875, together with the line South and East from Bischofshofen to Selzthal all by the KEB. From a junction on this latter line at Stainach Irdning a few miles short of Selzthal a KRB line was constructed

Northwards through the Salzkammergut by way of Bad Ischl and Gmunden through Attnang, Ried and the smiling district of Innkreis – a rolling land of low hills and alder fringed brooks – to Scharding on the KEB line from Linz to Passau.

The ill-fated war with Prussia in 1866 had demonstrated the usefulness of the KFNB, despite subsequent damage to it, in the transport of troops. It had already been the means of transporting troops to the siege of the rebel held Vienna in the late summer of 1848. Moreover the war and the seething unrest in Bohemia had shown how poor were the communications to the north west from Vienna. Nor, with the exception of the territories served by the KFNB, were matters much better east and north east of Vienna. Within a few years three railways had been promoted and built which altered the situation. These were the Franz Josefs Bahn, running from its own terminus in North Vienna to Gmund (on the present Austro Czech border) and on to Prague, the provincial capital of Bohemia, the Nord West Bahn to Znaim and Pardubitz – a line running roughly north west by north from Vienna – and the St EG (Staats Eisenbahn Gesellschaft) running from the Ostbahnhof in Vienna to Stadlau, Laa and Brunn (Brno) and also eastward into Hungary. The Franz Josefs Bahn was opened from Eggenburg to the north west by November 1869 and into the Vienna terminus the following June but the Nord West Bahn did not reach Vienna until June 1872. The line from the Ostbahnhof to Laa a.d. Thaya (which remains Austrian) was not opened until 24th November, 1870. Chopped off at the Czech border it is now part of the Vienna Schnellbahn as far as Hollabrunn and beyond that a somnolent country branch.

The early seventies were marked by an outburst of public improvements in Vienna made possible by the Imperial decree ordering the demolition of the fortifications enclosing the old city and the building of that noble thoroughfare the Ringstrasse, lined with some of the most notable of the capital's public and commercial buildings. The seventies were also marked in Vienna by the completion of the connecting railways linking the major railways running radially from the city.

Other lines belonging to the railway mania period were the Niederosterreichishe Sudwest Bahn (joining the east west main line at St Polten to the Sudbahn line at Leobersdorf, with branches) and the direct line from Villach to Triest (now crossed by the frontier South of Arnoldstein), a line from Steindorf (near Salzburg) north to the Bavarian frontier at Braunau (where it connected with the Bavarian Railways).

After the crash and loss of confidence in 1873 private capital became extremely shy of railway promotion. Apart from the three schemes already in being, mentioned earlier, namely the Niederosterreichische Sudwestbahn, the lines Salzburg-Bischofshofen-Wörgl-Selzthal and the line from Stainach to Scharding, railway construction in metropolitan Austria was restricted for a decade to minor links and branches.

Schemes such as the long canvassed western main line over the Arlberg to join Switzerland to Innsbruck, involving over six miles of tunnel at the summit alone had become unthinkable to private capital. Had it not been for the political revival of interest in State ownership c. 1877 it is doubtful if the railway would have been constructed at all. It was opened from Landeck through to Bludenz in September 1884 (for goods on the 6th and general traffic on the 21st). This was the last but one of the Austrian major trans-Alpine projects the last of which, the Tauernbahn linking Schwarzach to Spittal-Millstattersee and hence providing a direct route South from Salzburg to Villach·and Klagenfurt with their connections to Italy and present-day Yugoslavia, was opened in stages in September 1905 and July, 1909.

15

Another but secondary route (the Kremstalbahn) over the Alps runs from Linz South via Kremsmunster (reached 1881), Micheldorf (1883), Klaus (1888) and thence via Spital am Pyhrn to Selzthal (opened July, 1905). Formerly a lokalbahn link line (1893) from Wels to Kremsmunster Stift cut across the hypotenuse of the Wels-Linz-Kremsmunster trinagle theoretically making possible a more direct route from the Bavarian border at Braunau through to Bruck a.d. Mur and Graz but the character of the line made it unsuitable for through traffic.

The railways forming the wishbone transalpine routes St Valentin/Amstetten-Selzthal, St Michael, Villach-Tarvis-Pontafel/Laibach collectively formed the Kronprinz Rudolf Bahn.

The last railway promotion in Austria wholly by private capital was the 99 mile long Aspangbahn built by a Belgian company, the Cie Belge de Chemins de fer et d'Enterprises, from its own terminus in South East Vienna to Wiener Neustadt and from there on to Aspang, almost due south, with a branch from Sollenau westward to Puchberg from which a metre gauge rack-railway on the Abt system, under the same ownership, continued a further 9km to the summit of the Hochschneeberg where a hotel and observatory were built. It was intended originally, had not the money run out, to build a main line to Salonika on the Aegean Sea via Graz providing also an alternative route to that over the Semmering for traffic to Graz and Marburg (Maribor) but this enterprise never got beyond Aspang. In the end the link to Graz was completed by the state railways in 1910 with a line joining Aspang to Furstenfeld but never competed with the old Sudbahn route. The Aspangbahn itself was opened in stages during the summer and autumn of 1881 and the rack-railway up the Schneeberg in 1896.

During the eighties and nineties the branch line and secondary route network expanded under the encouragement of the lokalbahn legislation – roughly equivalent to the Light Railway Act, 1896 in Great Britain – which was aimed at preventing the drift of population from the countryside to the cities and to foreign countries, principally the United States, by improving communications with hitherto isolated villages and towns, allowing them access to markets which before they had been unable to reach by reason of transport problems. Local railway building had got off to a tame beginning under the laws of 1875 but in 1880 the Government gave much more sweeping relaxations of standards of construction and working in return for speed restrictions and also greater freedom to build lines on road side wastes. The response from promoters being still limited yet further amendments to the law were made in 1887, probably the most important of which was the provision that if the necessary capital was not otherwise forthcoming it might be provided by the central and provincial governments in equal shares. The restrictions upon laying lines on public roads were still further reduced and provided a speed limit of 28 kilometres an hour was adhered to sweeping reliefs were given in the provision of fencing, telegraph equipment and gates as well as in staffing. In addition powers were given in the Act for the government, at its discretion, to allow partial or total relief from taxation, from the duty to carry mails free, from police and supervisory charges, from stamp duties and from the obligation to stamp tickets and to allow the lokalbahn the use of junctions and stations at the main line connections either free or at advantageous rates. There was also provision for the State railway administration, if requested, to work local lines at less than cost.

The 1887 enactment was far more productive than its predecessors, resulting in the promotion of lines over a period of more than forty years, the last line of any consequence to be opened in the interwar years being the standard gauge Feldbach-Bad Gleichenberg, opened in June 1931 by the Styrian Provincial Railways.

The first lengthy railway to benefit was the 58km Muhlkreisbahn line from Urfahr (Linz) to Aigen/Schlägl opened in 1888. Aigen is in a tract of land that projects parson's nose fashion from the North border of Lower Austria and though a length of 39 miles might have been thought ambitious by our own light railway standards it fell short of the aims of the original promoter and builder, Count Lazarini, who had intended it to be linked to the Wels lokalbahn at Aschach on the Danube (opened, under the earlier acts, in 1886) and also to continue northward across the provincial border into what is now Czechoslovakia. Single tracked, steeply graded and rising 1230 feet between its independent terminal in North Linz and the summit at Rohrbach it was, and remains, an archetypal long country branch traversing, at a leisurely pace, entrancing scenery, largely ignored by visitors to Austria.

Curiously enough it was closely followed by the branch of the Hungarian State Railways serving Altpinkafeld in Burgenland. After the plebiscite of 1921 this was cut off like a tentacle without an octopus, isolated from contact with the general body of Austrian railways until the completion of a lokalbahn from Friedberg (on the Graz-Aspang route) eastward to Altpinkafeld, opening in November, 1925.

The lokalbahn law also gave rise to a number of 760cm lines the first of which, the Steyrtalbahn was opened from Garsten on the standard gauge line from St. Valentin to Kleinreifling (itself opened 1868/9) to Grunberg in August 1889 and for its whole length to Klaus in 1909. The Steyrtalbahn was, at the time of writing, still 100% steam worked, retaining four Krauss 0-6-2T of 1898–1902 from the NOLB and Bregenzerwaldbahn. It was followed closely by the first section of the now, regrettably, defunct Salzkammergut Lokalbahn, Salzburg to Bad Ischl, and the also defunct Innsbruck to Hall-in-Tyrol, mostly on roads.

The provincial government of Lower Austria was responsible for promoting a number of standard gauge local railways including the long route from Korneuberg via Mistelbach to Hohenau and the route crossing it from Stammersdorf (on the outskirts of Vienna) to Dobermannsdorf and also the rural branch from Retz to Drosendorf but many local lines were promoted by local private interests or by the Österreichische Lokaleisenbahn Gesellschaft, a beefed-up Austrian equivalent of Colonel Stephen's Light Railway Syndicate.

Another interesting secondary railway of the nineties, but no lokalbahn, was the combined rack and adhesion line over the roof of the Erzberg from Eisenerz to Vordenberg, opened in 1891, which with its steep grades, spirals and tunnels was, in steam days, surely one of the most fascinating of mountain railways, designed as it was not to carry a few coach loads of passengers to a mountain view point but thousands of tons of iron ore annually from the open cast mine to the steel works at Donawicz or for shipment to customers further afield. Freight was steam worked on this line until 1977 in part with original locomotives from the opening date.

The re-entry of the state into railway ownership was soon expanded by the accession of the Franz Josefs Bahn in 1884 but the KFNB was not taken over until 1907 and the Nord West Bahn and Ostbahn (StEG) did not follow until 1909.

The first railway in Austria opened as an electric line was the 1m gauge Modling-Hinterbruhl, 4.5km long, in the southern outskirts of Vienna opened in three sections in 1883, 1884 and 1885, followed by part of the inter-urban but standard gauge Badner Bahn in 1899 (the balance waited until 1906). Other electric pioneers were the Stubaitalbahn, metre gauge, from Innsbruck to Fulpmes, opened in 1904 and 18km long and the Montafonerbahn in the extreme west, a standard gauge line 13km long from Bludenz to Schruns. Other local railways followed. Of these perhaps the most interesting is the 760cm Mariazellerbahn which heads South from the Westbahn at St Polten through the Alpine foothills finally to penetrate the Alps themselves in a breathtaking series of spirals and tunnels to a terminus at Gusswerk 92km from St Polten. Opened as the Lokalbahn St Polten-Kirchberg a.d. Pielach-Marh Provincial Railways in stages from 1898, to 1907 it was taken over by the Lower Austrian Provincial Railways in 1908. It was originally worked by 0-8-0 locomotives with close coupled tenders, the survivors of which are still at work on the Waldviertalbahn in the North West corner of the province, but for which the precipitous stretches of their parent road proved frankly too much. The line was electrified in 1911 and the locomotives then put into service, albeit rebodied, still work the line.

The first main line conceived and built for electric traction was the mountainous Mittenwaldbahn from Innsbruck West station to the Bavarian frontier, over which it crosses near Scharnitz, to return to Austrian territory as the Ausserfernbahn which goes on to Reutte-in-Tyrol, all opened in 1913. The Pressburgerbahn, opened in 1914, eastward from Vienna along the South plain of the Danube to Pressburg (now Bratislava) was modelled on the American inter-urbans and was half-way between a tramway and a railway, though now a conventional railway operated by O.B.B.

Further railway development was stopped by the 1914/18 war at the end of which Austria was reduced to its present form with the exception, as related in the Introduction, of Burgenland which did not vote to join Austria until 1921.

The rump of the former kkSt.B was renamed the Deutsch Österreichischen Staatsbahnen but otherwise was not substantially amended. On 21st October, 1919 this title was shortened to Österreichische Staatsbahnen and on 1st April, 1921 changed again to Bundesbahnen Österreich (BBO).

Of the major railways only the western mainline to Salzburg, Innsbruck and the Vorarlberg remained intact though an appreciable part of the still company owned Sudbahn remained in Austria. The KFNB, St. EG, Franz Josefs Bahn and Nord West Bahn lines were all cut off by new frontiers at distances varying from 47 to 167km from Vienna, leaving extensive terminal facilities there grossly underused. Though a substantial mileage of the Sudbahn remained Austrian a considerable part had gone to Hungary and by no means negligible mileages to Yugoslavia and Italy. The independent Raab Odenburg and Ebenfurth Railway – a wishbone shaped line as will be seen from the map – was left inconveniently with the point of the bone in Hungary and the two branches in Austria. As if these circumstances did not pose difficulty enough there was also wrangling as to how the locomotives and rolling stock of the divided railways were to be allocated and, to complicate the matter further, there were both the political wrangling associated with the birth of the new Republic and the loss of the greater part of the coal resources upon which the railways had relied. With the gaining of Burgenland in 1921 came the difficulty of the severed lines from the new frontier at Rechnitz to Altpinkafeld and Oberndorf and other lesser complications of branches to Burgenland.

Because of the difficulties faced by the railways the Government of the Republic appointed Sir William Acworth (1850–1925), barrister and architect of the British grouping scheme to advise it upon the most suitable method of reorganising the Austrian system. Acworth recommended, predictably, that the railway should be grouped into a single Federal undertaking worked as a private enterprise but closely regulated as to the services to be provided and with stringent control of revenue. This revised arrangement took effect from 1st October, 1923, though the Sudbahn was not taken in until the following year and four mainline companies – the Aspangbahn, the Montafoner, the Raab Odenburg and Ebenfurth and the Graz-Koflach were left independent together with a number of minor undertakings, including the Steiermarkische Landesbahnen and the minor lines which now form the Stern and Hafferl empire.

The shortage of native coal produced great government interest, reflected in its policy toward the railways, in electricity from hydro-electric schemes. It was decided to carry out four major electrification schemes using single phase alternating current at $16^{2}/_{3}$ cycles 15000 volts, enabling through running with the Swiss and German systems to be carried on. The four schemes were:

1. The western main-line west from Innsbruck through the Arlberg to the border near Buchs, with the branch to Bregenz.
2. The line from Salzburg to Innsbruck with the branches from Worgl to Kufstein and from Innsbruck to the Italian frontier at Brenner.
3. The Salzkammergut line from Stainach-Irdning to Attnang Puchheim.
4. The Tauern line (Schwarzach-St Veit to Spittal-Millstattersee).

The electrification of the Arlberg and Tauern lines promised considerable relief in the working of the tunnels, particularly the Arlberg tunnel in which conditions with steam had become so unbearable that the installation of new mechanical ventilation would have been virtually inevitable had steam continued through it. Four railway owned hydro-electric power stations were built to serve these lines (Spullersee near Bludenz, Ruetz, south of Innsbruck, Stubach near Kitzbühel and Mallnitz, in the Tauern) with further supplies being drawn from the privately owned station at Achensee (to feed the Salzburg-innsbruck section and branches) and at Steeg (for the line south from Attnang-Puchheim). The first three of these electrifications were completed early in 1927 except for the line from Innsbruck to Brenner which was completed in October 1928 to a new station, Brennersee, wholly on Austrian soil from which cross frontier traffic was steam worked until the overhead was taken through to Brenner in April, 1934. The Tauern line was finished in 1935.

In 1933 the decision was taken in principle to continue the electric working from Salzburg east to Vienna and to electrify the route from Vienna Sud to Graz over the Semmering. Because of the difficulties of the international financial climate and the internal political problems of the country little had happened by the time of the Anschluss in March 1938.

The Austrian Federal Railways were amalgamated into the Reichsbahn on March 18th, 1938, passing under the control of the German Minister of Transport, Dr J. Dorpmuller, who was, ex officio, General Manager of the Reichsbahn though the former Federal Railway divisions were maintained and the head office departments in Vienna were kept as a sectional administration.

The electrification schemes which had been on the table at the time of the absorption remained unimplemented, not so much because of any inherent antipathy on the part of the Deutsche Reichsbahn (DRB) administration to the basic reasoning behind the schemes as because it had other priorities. Innovations by the DRB to the system itself were limited to the provision of link lines and avoiding lines. Doubtless these were undertaken primarily for war traffic but the work done had considerable permanent operational value. Amongst the places so treated from 1940 to 1943 may be named Feldkirch, Absdorf, Bruck a.d. Mur, Tulln, Goss, and St. Valentin. The avoiding line at Bruck, for instance, enabled traffic from

Graz to pass directly onto the line to Leoben and beyond without the necessity to enter Bruck station and reverse. Other wartime improvements were the Steinfelder relief line at Wiener Neustadt and the west relief line at Kledering on the approach to the Ostbahnhof.

The period of Reichsbahn management was responsible also for raising the permitted axle loadings for the first time above the 40,000lb mark on the principal main lines, a reform probably initiated to increase flexibility of working in the face of wartime demand rather than to meet any inherent need in Austria itself. Without the Anschluss or the war it is doubtful if any further major new locomotive types would have been put in hand in Austria but rather that the completion of the electrification would have been brought forward by a decade. As it was, however, the change of emphasis led to, inter alia, German classes 50, 44, 86, 52 and 42 working over Austrian lines.

Austrian metals formed the rail link with Germany's axis partner Italy until the latter's withdrawal from hostilities and separate armistice in 1943 whilst they were the way also into Yugoslavia and thence Greece besides being used as part of the rail access to Hungary, Rumania and Bulgaria. The junction towns – which, in several cases, were also industrial towns – thus became important targets and suffered accordingly. St. Pölten, Wiener Neustadt and Klagenfurt all underwent heavy allied bombing. The older Austrian locomotives classes with lighter axle loadings were plundered for locomotives to be used on more onerously load-restricted lines further east but this loss was offset by the drafting in of standard 2-10-0 Kriegsloks of Classes 42 and 52 many of which remained at the end of the war.

When the war ended in the defeat of the Reich the railways were left in a grievous state. At the time of the surrender it was estimated that 41% of the system was out of order – though it is not entirely clear whether the percentage refers to track miles or train miles.

From 27th April 1945 the railways, on reverting to Austrian control, were known as Osterreichische Staatseisenbahnen (Austrian State Railways) but as from August 1947 became Osterreichische Bundesbahnen (Austrian Federal Railways). The electrification programme was resumed on the western mainline and on the southern half of the Tauern route, reaching Villach in June 1950 and the Vienna Westbahnof a few days before Christmas 1951. Electric working over the Semmering, long talked about, was not brought into use, however, until May 1959, its tardiness providing the reason for the only post war steam express work of distinction (until 1956) achieved by Class 33 4-8-0's, followed by a short period of distinctly mediocre diesel locomotive working. The only post-war steam production for home use was a batch of German Class 42's built at Floridsdorf (Vienna) in 1945.

By 1969 with all major routes in the electrification programme complete with the exception of the line south from Graz to the frontier station at Spielfeld, the standard gauge steam locomotive stock had fallen to 435. By 1977 steam on standard gauge O.B.B. lines had come down to the Eisenerz rack and adhesion line but ceased that year. The Graz Koflacher Bahn went over to diesels at the end of 1977 leaving the Raab Odenburg Eberfurter as the sole user of standard gauge steam and even that on an occasional basis for service trains. Narrow gauge and rack-railway working presented rather more steam and in 1981 the Steyrtalbahn (760mm) was still 100% steam operated but main line steam had come to an end.

Chapter III
Locomotive practice up to 1890

Because of the resistance of the Emperor Franz I to the introduction of railways in his domains locomotive haulage on public railways in Britain and America had over ten years start over steam traction in Austria. Indeed it was only the KFNB which commenced operations in the 1830's at all and, with this exception, railway developments belonged to the 1840's.

Despite early similarities the respective paths of locomotive practice in Britain and America soon diverged. One might attempt to epitomise the differences by remarking that in Britain the terrain was subdued to suit the locomotive whilst in America the locomotive had to adapt itself to the terrain. Because also the labour of skilled artisans was scarcer and dearer in America the mechanical details of locomotives differed. America leaned to outside cylinders driving onto crank pins (where Britain increasingly relied upon inside cylinders and cranked axles) and to the use of wood or coal for firing at a time when British locomotives were designed for good quality coke whilst the indifferent track and severer curves of American lines encouraged the use of flexible trucks.

Understandably, in view of Riepl's admiration for Robert Stephenson and the construction and operation of the Liverpool & Manchester and its associated lines the KFNB began with a strongly Anglophile outlook and this established a tradition of which traces were still discernible at the end of the century. In this context it is hardly a surprise that the first two locomotives, "Austria" and "Moravia," delivered to the Nordbahn for use at the opening and for subsequent passenger traffic should have been 2-2-0's of Stephenson's "Mercury" type with inside cylinders and gab motion. It was "Austria" that had the honour of hauling the opening train in November, 1837. The goods locomotives were three Stephenson-built 0-4-2's "Samson", "Hercules" and "Vulcan". All were shipped to Triest and drawn by horses to Vienna. It may be wondered that they were not routed via the navigable sections of the Rhine and Danube which would have delivered them almost on the doorstep of the owning company but though, by this route, the overland portage between the limits of navigation of the two rivers would have been shorter than the long land haul from Triest it would have involved multiple crossings of frontiers with the concomitant of tolls at each whereas by being landed at Triest they were on Austrian territory from the outset. Though of the same wheel arrangement and ordered at the same time the three locomotives differed in dimensions, except driving wheel diameter (1372mm in each), and the "Vulcan" was an altogether larger and more powerful machine. Though the cylinder diameter in the first two was identical (305mm) the stroke in "Hercules" was 457mm against 406mm in "Samson" whilst in "Vulcan" the cylinders were 317×457mm, the heating surface in the latter locomotive being 44.642m² against 38.441m² and 44.091m² in "Samson" and "Hercules" respectively. Subsequently Stephenson delivered the "Vindobona" a 2-2-2 with outside sandwich frame and short inside frame. So far as the Nordbahn was concerned this locomotive was a vast improvement on and set the tide of opinion against the four-wheeled "Austria" and "Moravia" but it was not until the French disaster at Meudon-Bellvue on the Paris-Versailles Railway caused by the failure of an axle in a four wheeled locomotive in May 1842 that the Imperial Chancellery issued a decree forbidding their use in Austria though the two examples concerned were not finally broken up until 1849.

"Vindobona" was followed by two Belgian 2-2-2's "Saturn" and "Mercur" from the works of John Cockerill of Seraing which turned out to be somewhat under-cylindered and these in turn by four further Stephenson 2-2-2's – "Jupiter", "Gigant", "Concordia" and "Bruna", of improved design. Rebuilt in 1853 the last of these, "Jupiter" was in existence until 1861, though none were used after 1856.

The next order to England for a locomotive fell to Jones, Turner & Evans of Newton-le-Willows, again for a 2-2-2 basically in the Stephenson mould but marginally larger – the driving wheels 1870mm against 1829 in the "Jupiter" type and the total heating surface 42.6m^2 against 41.144m^2 in the slightly earlier engines but a more decisive move to a large engine was made in the "Bucephalus" delivered by Charles Tayleur (later Vulcan Foundry) of Newton-le-Willows in 1839. Here the cylinders were 338×454mm against 305×457mm in the "Jupiter" type, the driving wheels were 1847mm diameter, against 1829mm and the total heating surface 49.1m^2. In 1839 "Bucephalus" performed the not inconsiderable feat of taking an express from Gänserndorf to the terminus in Vienna at an average speed of 62.5km/h.

Whilst Mathias Schönerer, the engineer of the Vienna-Raab railway, was engaged, in 1837, upon setting up the railway's locomotive shops beside the Sud-bahnhof in Vienna he appointed a British engineer, John Haswell (1812–1897), to be works manager. Haswell came to railway work from the service of William Fairbairn & Sons who began building fixed and ships engines in 1817. Whilst in Vienna supervising the erecting of Fairbairn machinery in the Vienna-Raab shops he was noticed by Mathias Schönerer and invited to undertake the management of the shops when completed. He brought with him to the position two important attributes, firstly a thorough knowledge of and grounding in engineering practice as it then existed in the leading firms in England and secondly an open mind ready to weigh the work of others on its merits. Haswell subsequently had a distinguished career in Austria, accorded acclaim and honour as the father of Austrian locomotive building and a pillar of the professional establishment of German speaking Austria.

As British manufacturers had been profiting from the absence of an Austrian locomotive building industry so too their counterparts in the United States had reached a position from which they too were able to compete for sales to the European mainland. The firm which had the earliest and most extended success in broaching the European market was that of Norris Brothers of Philadelphia. With the impending opening of the Vienna-Raab Railway these American influences came to bear their part in shaping Austrian practice.

The American built 4-2-0 "Philadelphia" was delivered in November 1837 to the Vienna-Raab, having been ordered by Mathias Schonerer during a visit to the United States, and was basically similar to the Norris locomotives on the Bristol & Gloucester Railway and to more numerous examples set to work in the United States.

The Norris firm had begun locomotive manufacture in 1831 and by 1840 had achieved a total of about 135 of which 94 were at work in North America. About the year 1837 it began a sales campaign aimed at selling locomotives to European railways. In this effort there was a considerable measure of success in relation to the total locomotive stud of Eruope at the time. Within a period of nine years to 1846 thirty-three Norris locomotives had been sold on this side of the Atlantic. The characteristics of these locomotives were a leading bogie, bar frame, outside inclined cylinders driving a single driving axle placed far back, gab motion and the use of a boiler with a circular haystack firebox and long barrel. Anyone wishing to view a lineal descendant of a Norris has merely to step off the train at Pöchlarn on the Linz-Vienna main line, walk a short distance westward down the station approach and view OBB

No. 770.86 (ex Bavarian State Railways 178.84) built in 1909 and now displayed on a pedestal outside a block of flats – a 2-4-0 it is true but with the Norris influence plainly displayed and built into it seventy-two years after "Philadelphia", arrived at Triest in the Austrian vessel "Cupido" early in 1838 and was delivered to Vienna, after the same troublesome overland journey behind horses, in April. Gölsdorf notes that it was tried on a temporary track near Meidling, now in the southern outskirts of Vienna, where the Philadelphia – brücke is the monument to the event.

"Philadelphia" was soon followed by the very similar "Columbus" for the Nordbahn and by "Laxenburg" and "Raab" for the Vienna-Raab. In these engines 267×406 cylinders were used with 37.63m^2 of heating surface in the "Columbus". These dimensional advantages, coupled with the fact that Norris engines habitually ran at about 50% above the nominal boiler pressure gave them a pronounced operational advantage over two axle Stephenson locomotives. It may well be argued – and with truth – that the latter were an obsolete type when supplied but nevertheless they were what the makers had chosen to manufacture and sell. Despite the absence of finish in many of their parts the Norris engines were well thought of and, for their time, long lasting. "Columbus", for instance, ran until 1852, by which time its design was long outdated.

The later British imports, such as the big 0-4-2 "Vulcan", came out much better when compared with the Americans but they tended to suffer from the failure of their wrought iron cranked axles in the bitter winter cold. Tyre fractures plagued both types but a point chalked up against the British built engines was the difficulty of keeping them supplied with fuel of high enough quality to suit their smaller grates and fireboxes.

Norris type locomotives consequently took a firm hold upon the Austrian scene. Not only were further engines ordered from Philadelphia (to a total of some fourteen) but also manufacture in Austrian works began to gather impetus.

John Haswell, installed at the head of the Vienna-Raab shops, turned out the "Wien" a 4-2-0 of Norris configuration, though not of Norris dimensions, in 1841 and the following year Wenzel Guenther who had worked with Haswell on the Vienna-Raab set up his own works at Wiener Neustadt where he began operations by turning out six Norris type locomotives for the Northern State Railway, followed by another eleven with larger cylinders but smaller driving wheels.

Guenther took a further important step in 1844 when he supplied the "Koloss" and "Elephant", to the KFNB in which he combined the general Norris profile with the 2-4-0 wheel arrangement from which it was a logical step to Haswell's 4-4-0 "Steinbruck" of 1848, now preserved in the Vienna Technical Museum. To some extent Guenther's "Koloss" and "Elephant" broke the true Norris tradition by having the relatively long coupled wheelbase of 2400mm out of a total wheelbase of 3529mm

A third exponent of the Norris type in Austria, George Sigl (1811 to 1887) opened his works in the northern suburbs of Vienna, in the area between what are now the Ring and the Gurtel, near the present Wahringer Strasse in the 9th District, in 1842 and in 1844 William & Octavius Norris, presumably worried at the plagiarism of their designs, set up a works of their own in Vienna, as neighbours to Sigl. They supplied three locomotives to the Northern State Railway (now in Czechoslovakia) in 1846 and three ("Orpheus", "Aeolus" and "Ulysses") to the KFNB in 1846/7. The Norris enterprise, already sorely beset by the local competition, did not survive the Viennese revolt and subsequent siege the following year (1848) and the works itself was taken over by Sigl and joined to his own establishment next door. Like George England at Hatcham Ironworks in London Sigl was in the curious situation of having no railway line near his works in North Vienna and so in 1867 he purchased Guenther's business and works at Wiener Neustadt 50km south of Vienna on the line to Gloggnitz. The three Viennese Norris locomotives for the KFNB enjoyed relatively long working lives before being sold out of service in 1866. The three Vienna built Norris engines for the Northern State Railway had as running mates on that line, a group of eight rather curious variants of the Norris concept from the hand of Koechlin of Mulhouse (Alsace) in which the cylinders (409mm×630mm) were brought down to a horizontal position with the leading cover immediately below the buffer beam and the centre of the bogie pushed back under the boiler barrel. The driving wheels were small for a Norris derivative (1262mm) and the typical Norris haystack firebox, dignified even if, by the mid 1840's, obsolescent, was exaggerated into a high cylindrical affair of the type much beloved over many years by French makers of agricultural portable engines. Despite the faintly unpromising appearance these locomotives presented – that of a Norris crossed with a Stephenson long-boiler locomotive – they had link motion reversing gear as compared to the gab motion of the true Norris trio whilst one was fitted with Meyer supplementary expansion valves on each main valve.

A further Norris derived type contemporary with all the foregoing was the KFNB 4-4-0 series of the "Aetna" type supplied by John Cockerill of Seraing in which an otherwise strongly Norris design had a boiler with a round topped firebox. In the hands of Haswell the Norris 4-4-0 endured in progressively developed form and increased dimensions until 1857 at the end of which period there was far more of Haswell than of Norris in it. Latter examples used link motion reversing gear, had horizontal cylinders and slide valves inside the frames. Moreover Haswell in latter examples employed a two axle radial truck instead of the swivelling centre pin truck, a piece of pioneering for which he has only belatedly been accorded credit. In later examples also Haswell used a boiler with a round topped firebox to which pattern many of the earlier products were brought into line on reboilering.

"Steinbruck" was built by Haswell in 1848 for the Wien-Gloggnitzer Bahn – soon to become part of the Sudbahn – for whom it worked until 1864 but the greater part of its life was spent upon the Graz-Koflacher Bahn which runs west and northwest from Graz to the great open cast brown coal deposit at Koflach and divides at Lieboch to run south from there to Wies-Eibiswald. As their No. 827, renamed "SODING" it remained in use and latterly in store until 1908 when, by great good fortune, it was recognised as an historic machine and marked down for preservation.

In the "Adlitzgraben" and "Kaiserbrunn" (4-4-0's) for the Wien-Gloggnitzer Bahn in 1844 Haswell used, for the first time in Austria, compensating beams between the springing of the two driven axles, an arrangement adopted about the same time by Cockerill in Belgium and Rogers in the United States. These two locomotives, for passenger work, had 368×579mm cylinders, a boiler pressure of 6 Atmospheres, a heating surface of 81.80 square metres and 1422mm driving wheels (the same diameter, incidentally, as in the 1846 0-6-0 "Fahrafeld" for the same railway) but the mixed traffic 4-4-0 "Bruck" built for the railway in 1846 had only 1264mm driving wheels, allied to 403×579mm cylinders and a pressure of 6.3 Atmospheres. The heating surface in the "Bruck" had increased correspondingly to 83 square metres but even more so in the "Fahrafeld" in which it was no less than 135.9 square metres, largely because of the very long boiler barrel and overhung firebox.

The locomotives of Haswell, Guenther and Sigl shared this characteristic of a large firebox placed behind the driven axle or axles, an essential step in providing the size of grate necessary to enable the locomotives to run upon indigenous wood or brown coal. In this it has been suggested that Haswell, who could hardly have failed to have been in touch with events in locomotive building in England, may have copied Stephensons' patented long-boiler locomotives, with his two junior contemporaries following suit. There may have been some truth in this, though it has perhaps been demonstrated in the opening paragraphs of this Chapter that Norris was a more likely source of inspiration, but insofar as imports from Britain continued to grace the Austrian scene, particularly on the Anglophile KFNB the locomotives had nothing of the long-boiler type about them being mainly 2-2-2's. These included a notably unsuccessful example by G. & J. Rennie of London delivered in 1839 which had to be rebuilt locally within four years of delivery – though, in fairness, it must be noted that it then continued in service until 1865 – and a block of four, "Phoenix", "Meteor", "Titan" and "Pluto", from Sharp Roberts & Co. (Works Nos. 123, 124, 126 and 128) in 1841 incorporating the features which endeared Sharpies to the operating departments of British railways – reliability, economy and astonishing speed.

One visual feature of the Sharpies assimilated into local usage was the dome with classically fluted Sharp Roberts encasing and spring balance safety valve in the top but another and more important feature to be assimilated was the outside frame. Only on the KFNB was the 2-2-2 a lasting type. Of these the 1a's appeared from Sigl's works in 1862, the 1b's (Nos. 84–87) in 1871 from Hannover and the final batch (88–91) from Floridsdorf in 1873. The typical locomotive of the KFNB, however, in the fifties, sixties and seventies, large wheeled for passenger working and small wheeled for freight, was the short wheel-based 2-4-0 with wide firebox placed behind the rear coupled axle, the horizontal centre line of the boiler well below 2m above rail level – the 1700 to 1800mm height range being commoner – and a total wheelbase of about 3.50m. There were exceptions to this rule, notably the IIb1's rebuilt in 1882/3 from the 2-2-2's of Series 1a in which the firebox was between the coupled axles and the wheelbase correspondingly increased to 4584mm, a metamorphosis which also overtook the 1b's producing a configuration on which English eyes might have alighted with much less sense of affront than on some of the short wheelbased, inside framed 2-4-0's.

Probably the most important event of the 1840's was the decision of the government in 1842 to proceed with the construction of the line southward from Gloggnitz over the Semmering Pass to Murzzuschlag. The civil engineer responsible for the survey and choice of route was Carl von Ghega who already had the KFNB to his credit and by 1844 he had reached a final decision on the course of the line. Nevertheless the doubts engendered by the sheer grandeur of the venture led to intense public and departmental debate both as to its practicability at all and, aside from that, the feasibility of working it, as Ghega envisaged, by locomotives. It was left to the government of the newly enthroned Franz Josef I to extinguish the debate under the first heading by a decision to proceed.

Although the Semmering is the lowest of the great Austrian Alpine passes (an altitude of about 900m compared with twice that over the Arlberg) the railway crossing of it was an undertaking of great daring for 1848. The line rises 441m from Gloggnitz to the summit south of Alter Semmering tunnel at 898m with a ruling gradient of 2½% uncompensated for 31 chain curves. Apart from the justly celebrated two storey Kalte Rinne viaduct 184m long and 46m above the valley bed below it incorporates sixteen other viaducts and the same number of tunnels. In all the line is 41.8km from Gloggnitz to Murzzuschlag, much of it at 1 in 50 and 9km at 1 in 40.

The Austrian Institute of Engineers and Architects stated publicly the opinion that the only feasible option of working it would be cable haulage which was in direct opposition to the views of von Ghega who, in turn, enjoyed strong support in the German-language technical press. It was one organ of the latter (the *Stuttgarter Eisenbahn Zeitung*) which appears to have first carried the suggestion of a practical trial though it may well have been Riepl's appreciation of the value of the Rainhill Trial twenty years before that brought about the decision of the Ministry of Transport to stage a competitive performance trial for motive power for the Semmering.

The principal conditions laid down for entries were as follows. They had to be capable of hauling a train weight (apart from the weight of the engine and tender, if used,) of 140 imperial tons, the maximum wheel loading not to be greater than 7000kg and the boiler pressure no more than 7 atmospheres. These requirements were paired to an overall height and width of 4.72m and 2.84m respectively and a stopping distance, when running light, of 152m, from 30km/hr to rest. Of seven entrants who intimated their intention to take part four actually delivered engines for trial at the end of July, 1851 namely Maffei of Munich, Cockerill of Seraing, Wenzel Guenther of Wiener Neustadt and the Vienna-Raab Railway (Haswell) of Vienna. The winner of the 20,000 florin prize – in return for which the locomotive became the property of the railway – was Maffei's "Bavaria". Despite its high exhibtion performance "Bavaria", an eight coupler in whose design the front four driving wheels, which had provision for lateral movement, were linked by chains on the horizontal centre line to the rear four driven wheels, never turned a wheel in revenue earning service because of it being found in practice impossible to overcome the problems of stretching and breakage in the chains. Had roller chains then been invented the outcome might have been more satisfactory though, even in the twentieth century era of high performance roller chains, chains and main line steam locomotives were never paired successfully on a commercial scale. It was the fate of "Bavaria" to be written off against experience, the boiler being taken from the frame and used for stationary work in the Sudbahn shops at Marburg (Maribor). As to boiler the design was conventional and viewed elevationally the locomotive, at first glance, appeared to be an 0-8-0 with unequal spacing of the axles. Closer examination would have shewn, however, that the third axle, on which the cylinders drove, and the fourth axle were rigid in the horncheeks and coupled by conventional side rods but that the leading four driven wheels were in a separate flexibly mounted truck. Though these two truck axles were coupled together by side rods they were yoked to the third axle by a chain and sprockets on the centre line. The tender had six wheels of the same diameter as the main locomotive, coupled by side rods and chain driven from the fourth axle in the same way as the leading truck. No effective means were provided for keeping chains and sprockets in truth and this resulted in frequent breakages which set at naught the otherwise attractive capabilities of the engine in load haulage and adhesion on steep gradients.

"Seraing", John Cockerills entry, by using a double ended boiler and two two axle flexible powered trucks anticipated some of the characteristics of Fairlie's rather later design. He added to his difficulties by using inside cylinders and motion which, taken in conjunction with the presence inside the frames of the paraphanalia of the articulated suspension produced an almost intolerable congestion of machinery. There is said to have been a difficulty, shared by Fairlie locomotives, of maintaining the flexible joints of the steam pipes in a steam tight condition and this, leading to waste of steam, taken with perhaps a less than adequate generation capacity in the double ended boiler marked down this locomotive also as a commercial failure by a small margin. It was intended to run with a four wheeled water tank.

Guenther's "Wiener Neustadt" was again a two truck articulated locomotive but with a single ended boiler. The designer provided better accessibility to the engine parts by the use of outside cylinders, though with inside valve gear but, like Cockerill, failed to solve the problems inherent in the flexible joints of the steam pipes.

Haswell's "Vindobona", least noticed – at least by the press and public – at the trials proved to be, in every practical aspect, the most useful of the entrants. In it Haswell used a boiler with a flat crowned firebox (anticipating Belpaire), outside cylinders and a more or less conventional 0-8-0 wheel arrangement, achieving accommodation to sharp track curvature by placing the first three axles at very close centres, the third pair of wheels being flangeless, and a fourth axle behind the firebox, giving the appearance of a 0-10-0 with the fourth axle omitted. In the design Haswell incorporated provision for braking by using the cylinders as compressors and providing a by-pass valve enabling the air so compressed for braking purposes to be drawn direct from atmosphere rather than through the gritty blastpipe aperture. Braking of this type was later used by Le Chatelier and by Riggenbach in his rack locomotives. By placing the steam take-off and regulator valve high up in a large dome Haswell improved the chances of working with dry steam whilst at the same time maximising the ability to keep the water level high on gradients, one of the more desirable attributes of the hay-stack fireboxes used on the Norris locomotives.

The "Vindobona" was the least drastically innovative of the entries at Semmering but, so far as Austrian practice was concerned, such innovations as it contained were the most enduring. This is not, in any way, to belittle the efforts of the other entrants, though the chain coupled "Bavaria" was perhaps the least valuable of the prize locomotives. None of the entrants, or at least the flexible first three, fulfilled exactly the postulates of the competition (though they all had the required tractive capacity). Despite its practicality the "Vindobona" succeeded largely by ignoring the letter of the requirements. When the adjudicating committee presented its report on September 12th, 1851 it included the recommendation that a further locomotive should be designed and built which, it was hoped, would obviate the disadvantages of the competitors.

The task of designing this locomotive was assigned to Baron Wilhelm Engerth, (1819–84) departmental chief engineer of the Austrian Ministry of Industry. Born at Pless in the Prussian part of Silesia Engerth had become, as a comparatively young man, Professor of Machine Construction at Graz University, from which post he had moved on to the Ministry of Industry. Engerth is said originally to have experimented by a reconstruction of the ill-fated "Bavaria" from which he produced the design of the entirely distinct type of articulated locomotive known since by his name. Initially two tank locomotives of this design were ordered – one from Kessler of Esslingen and the other from Cockerill. The three leading axles were closely spaced and carried in the main frames which were inside. Outside cylinders and Gooch-type valve gear were used. The rear end of the locomotive was carried on a flexible motor truck with outside frames running on two axles, coupled by outside rods. Drive was transmitted from the rear-most of the three fixed coupled axles to the leading axle of the flexible truck by a train of gear comprising a gear on each axle and a third on an intermediate shaft. The intermediate shaft was of square cross section where it carried the gear and provision was made for taking the flexible truck out of drive by sliding the gear sideways. After the initial designs were approved a batch of 26 was put in hand and eventually over a hundred were in service, not all with the coupling gear. Though the locomotives as originally designed were magnificent load movers on straight or lightly curved track it soon became apparent that, despite the teeth of the gears being tapered in three directions they were still unable to accommodate fully the relative movements imposed by actual operation and frequent breakage of teeth became a problem whilst, in one or two extreme cases, derailments of the locomotive occurred because the interlocking of the teeth had prevented movement of the rear truck. It was found, however, that the three directly driven axles could transmit sufficient power to deal with the 140 tonne loads with which they were required to cope. When they came under the administration of the privately owned Sudbahn attempts to make them fully workable in their geared form were abandoned and they were rebuilt from 1860 onwards as straightforward eight coupled engines with ballast weights at the rear to give satisfactory weight distribution, enabling them to be used for heavier trains at slower speeds viz 11Km/hour instead of 16. Engerth locomotives enjoyed a decade of attention and were used on other railways than the Semmering – in Greater Austria, Switzerland and Belgium. Despite many endeavours in the ensuing seventy years no European railway succeeded in getting a successful geared locomotive to work until in Germany the Luttermöller system of 1917 provided gear coupling of single axles at the front and or rear end of a group of rod-coupled axles and this was mechanically perfect as well as radially adaptable.

Whatever Engerth's motives in ordering the locomotives from foreign builders as opposed to the nascent Austrian locomotive building establishments the decision provoked a very bitter response from Haswell who doubtless considered that in building the "Vindobona" (the Roman name for Vienna) he had provided ample proof of the abilities of his works and himself. Haswell was never the owner of the works he managed but, like Francis Webb at Crewe, regarded it, nevertheless, as "his" works and treated Engerth's action as a personal affront which he never forgave. One can, perhaps, sympathise with Engerth when he shrank from entrusting the detailed development of his cherished schemes to a locomotive builder who made no secret of his lack of faith in articulated locomotives but it must surely have been a calculated slight when he caused the whole of the production batch of twenty six locomotives to be ordered abroad, although the official explanation was overstretching of the Austrian builders of the time.

Engerth's decision so infuriated Haswell that he forbade him entry to the works. In 1860, to Haswell's chagrin, Engerth was appointed general manager of the Staats Eisenbahn Gessellschaft, and thus Haswell's superior. An early act by which Engerth exerted his authority over the testy Scot was by ordering the works to build four ten-coupled tank engines on a modified version of his system. The engines were, indeed, built there but Haswell ignored them and Engerth was obliged to supervise their building himself with the assistance of Pius Fink. This curious feud between two eminent and knowledgeable, albeit opinionated, men lasted another twenty years until Engerth retired.

Subsequently it fell to Haswell to design the type of locomotive which was the mainstay of Alpine railway working for many years. Taking a close coupled 0-8-0 he placed on it a long boiler of ample capacity with a large firebox entirely behind the rear coupled axle, using outside cylinders and motion and giving flexibility by providing lateral movement in the journals and bearings of the end axles, accommodated by lengthened crank pins. Such locomotives were liable to hunt at any but the most moderate speeds but high speed was never a feature of mountain freight work. On the most severe curves the permanent way departments were known also to ease flange friction by making the rails marginally wide to gauge, a practice which received at least one thundering denunciation in the pages of *The Engineer*. A locomotive of this initial series from the St. EG Works (as the Vienna-Raab had become) (works number 303 of 1855) was exhibited at the Paris Exhibition in that year, earned a gold medal there and was purchased by the Midi Railway of France, on which it ran as number 301. It ended its working life, rebuilt as a side tank locomotive, shunting at an ironworks in Perigord in 1913.

In a period of eighteen years Austria had progressed, therefore, from the use of an imported Stephenson "Mercury" type 2-2-0 for its first main-line to the state of having a native locomotive building industry capable of producing advanced – and medal-winning – heavy locomotives destined for a useful life of fifty-eight years. The importance of the Semmering trials and their aftermath was not so much in the patterns of locomotive which they engendered – though features of these were of lasting influence – as in the fact that it had been conclusively demonstrated by the trials that the working of steeply graded railways, up to 1 in 40, by simple adhesion was entirely practicable. Had this not been demonstrated there can be little doubt that the development of the other major trans-Alpine routes would have been set back by many years or would perhaps have been drawn into the hampering by-way of rope haulage.

In a lesser plane but nonetheless interesting is another development which took place in Wiener Neustadt. The building of the great military establishment at Fischau near Wiener Neustadt involved the haulage of large tonnages of stone, for which purpose a three foot gauge (948mm) light railway was built for which Johann Zeh (of Guenthers) designed three 2-4-2 side tank locomotives with 316mm×421mm outside cylinders 948mm driving wheels and a working pressure of 6 atmospheres. The success of this wheel arrangement may well have led to its adoption for a series of locomotives three years later on the Tiroler Staatsbahn, to which notice will be given a little later, and it further led to the design, also by Zeh of the side-tank locomotives used in 1855 and 1856 for the conversion of the 1106mm gauge Lambach-Gmunden line to steam operation – a 4-4-0 design of which ten were built (Nos. 1–10 inclusive) for passenger working and a 2-6-2 for goods. In the latter the cylinder dimensions – and probably the actual cylinder design – was as in the Fischau 2-4-2's but in the passenger engine the diameter was reduced to 250mm. In each case the boiler pressure was increased to 6.7 atmospheres. The 4-4-0's had 948mm driving wheels as in the Fischau locomotives but the 2-6-2 had wheels only 790mm in diameter. One of these locomotives, 4-4-0 No. 4 "Gmunden" came back into the hands of the Wiener Neustadt Works when it was superseded in 1882 and was presented to the Vienna railway museum where it is still on exhibition.

Despite the early flowering of the eight coupled types on the lines running south and south east from Vienna four and six coupled locomotives remained the Austrian norm during the latter 1850's. Apart from the Wien-Gloggnitz and Semmering lines, which passed from state to private ownership, as the Sudbahn, at the end of 1858, the Kaiser Ferdinand Nordbahn, and the St. EG, successor of the Vienna-Raab, most of whose respective mileages in any event were outside the limits of modern Austria, the other major railway in operation in the late fifties was the Kaiserin Elizabeth (which reached Linz from Vienna in 1858).

The KEB was faithful, for a number of years, to the 2-4-0 type for passenger work. Their class I (later Class 12 of the State Railways) with 420×632mm outside cylinders, 1580mm diameter drivers and a working pressure of 7 atmospheres was supplied to them by Haswell (St. EG) and Guenther. They were remarkable, in locomotives intended for main line passenger work, in having a total wheelbase of only 3.425m out of a total length (excluding buffers) of 7.875m. With inside frames, vestigial splashers, no running plates and absence of cabs they contrived to look very spartan but were prodigious workers. After they came into state ownership they were provided with roomy cabs and vacuum brakes but otherwise not much altered, in which guise they soldiered on until well into this century.

The goods work on the KEB was undertaken by long boilered 0-6-0's. In these the cylinders, whilst retaining the 632mm stroke of the 2-4-0's were increased in bore to 457mm, the boiler pressure remaining at 7 atmospheres though the total heating surface was increased from 131.60 to 138.12 square metres. The wheelbase was even shorter (3.16m) than in the 2-4-0's, the overall length being 235mm shorter at 7.64m. Early examples had a weatherboard only, turned over at the top but later examples had a reasonably presentable cab and all were provided eventually with very creditable cabs. With subsequent developments these 0-6-0's were the main source of freight power on the KEB both in private and later state ownership for the remainder of the century and many lasted well into this century though the earliest to survive into BBO ownership dated from 1860. One of the later examples (kkStB 47-54) was selected in 1901 to be the first to carry a Brotan boiler. Brotan was a senior engineer of the State Railways and his boiler was used widely in Hungary but not in Austria proper but, in any case, it belongs chronologically to the next chapter and will be discussed there.

The fashion for long boilers and short wheelbases in 0-6-0 tender locomotives was reflected on the KFNB in 1869. At an overall length of 7.394m they were not radically different from the KEB examples but the wheelbase was only 3.003m. The cylinders were 632×434mm but the pressure was 9 atmospheres, the boiler heating surface being brought down from 138.12 square metres in the KEB engines to 120.00 square metres on the KFNB though the grate area in fact increased from $1.29m^2$ to $1.70m^2$.

Of the lines which went to form the private Sudbahn in September, 1858, the greater number fell, territorially speaking, outside the scope of this book. One of the constituent railways, however, which qualified for inclusion in these pages, the Tiroler Staatsbahn, which began building its lines (Kufstein-Innsbruck and Bozen to Verona) in 1850 was not opened, in fact, until two months after its undertaking was handed over to the Sudbahn but at the time of the change of ownership locomotives for the commencement of traffic had already been built and were in store, comprising eighteen small-wheeled outside cylinder 2-4-2's of 1857 (which became Sudbahn numbers 252–269 inclusive in Series 7) and eight Engerth locomotives for freight dating from 1856. These latter took the Sudbahn numbers 593–600 inclusive.

The 2-4-2 was never a numerous type on the railways of the Empire. Only the St. EG. used the wheel arrangement on a wider scale, adopting virtually in toto the successful and long-lived design of the Paris-Orleans Railway for building both in their own works and by outside builders. The original and thoroughly French design dated from 1883 and when the St. EG. came into the Austrian state fold in 1909 (its Hungarian lines had been nationalised in 1891) twenty-six of these haughty Gallic thoroughbreds passed to the kk St. B in whose designation scheme they became Class 5. With them came also two further and slightly later 2-4-2 locomotives of Class 105 in which, if foreign leanings were to be sought, these were to be found more in Anglicised than in Gallicised external details. They survived into BBO ownership after the 1914/18 war but were withdrawn progressively in the early twenties, the last three running until 1927. With 460×650mm cylinders, 2120mm driving wheels and a working pressure of 9 atmospheres a St. EG. 2-4-2 was a powerful and fast machine.

The eighteen sixties and first years of the seventies saw the greatest period of growth in the railway system of the Austrian homeland. The Kron Prinz Rudolf Bahn, opened in stages between 1868 and 1877, began its working life with two classes of outside cylindered outside framed 0-6-0 tender locomotives built by Sigl, the earlier examples coming from the old works in the ninth district but later examples from Wiener Neustadt. The first batch lasted until the first world war as Class 929 of the kk St. B and the last example ran until 1923 but the second series which became Class 34 were not withdrawn until 1927/29. Out of deference to the Alpine and sub-Alpine terrain in which much of the system was situated the wheel diameter was 1210mm compared with 1300mm on the KEB locomotives from the same maker.

The KRB also had two batches of 2-4-0 long-boiler tender engines in 1870 and 1873 respectively with outside cylinders and frames but inside valve gear, no splashers and only the most rudimentary of running plates. Their appearance was archaic even for 1873 but they were nevertheless extremely useful locomotives for secondary work and had working lives of upwards of forty years, the final survivor lasting in traffic until 1923. Another long lived class of 2-4-0's were the Class 121's originally built as the KFNB Class ND – which numbered 42 in all – between 1867 and 1873 again of the long-boilered close coupled type. Unlike those of the KEB and KRB they were, however, inside framed. With 1266mm driving wheels and 382×615mm cylinders they were intended when new purely for goods work but, being kind to light track and sharp curves, they appeared on all kinds of minor passenger duties in their latter years. The class survived almost intact to the 1918 division of locomotives when, despite the fact that they they had mostly worked outside the Austrian homeland twenty-six were handed over to the Austrian Federal Railways and it was not until 1927 that the last was withdrawn. Despite its early use of the Norris type 4-2-0's and 4-4-0's the KFNB had displayed an interest in the alternative of the 2-4-0 as early as 1843 when Guenther delivered "Koloss" and "Elephant". Despite its unusual features – which included a piston rod some 2000mm long and a coupled wheelbase of 2400mm where many of the contemporary Norris type 4-4-0's were using only 1400mm – Koloss had a long life on the KFNB from which it was sold in 1871 to become a construction locomotive on the Weyer – Rottenmann line of the Kron Prinz Rudolf Bahn. The probability is that it was found that a 2-4-0 rode as well, particularly in freight or slow passenger service, as a 4-4-0 with a Norris-type four wheeled leading truck such as the contemporary"Donau"class.

These latter locomotives were delivered by Cockerill in 1844 as 4-4-0's but after a disastrous accident to"Donau"itself on 26th June, 1851, in which a broken leading axle led to the explosion of the boiler, first"Donau"and then the other seven fo the series were rebuilt as 2-4-0's with larger boilers. The driving wheel diameter in this class was 1264mm and the coupled wheelbase only 1400mm out of an overall length (apart from buffers) of 8865mm which cannot have made for anything other than a very rough ride even at the speeds of Austrian stopping passenger trains of the 1850's. A driving wheel diameter of 1264mm was used by the KFNB for 2-4-0's intended for goods work, 1580mm for intermediates and 1897mm for express locomotives. The goods and intermediate classes were, without exception and unlike the locomotives of its neighbours, inside framed and outside cylindered, though with the valve gear inside the frames.

For express work Maffei delivered in 1855 the "Telegraph" type 2-4-0's with inside cylinders and outside frames, the trailing coupled axle behind the firebox. Probably with 395×619mm cylinders they found themselves not over supplied with steam from their original boilers, pressed to only 5.4 atmospheres and with a total heating surface of 102.7 square metres but when reboilered with 112.9 square metres of heating surface and a pressure of 6.5 atmospheres they were fast and stylish machines. Dr Karl Gölsdorf called them the "volkommene Schnellzugtype", (the perfect express type) and they were indeed attractive locomotives. From the point of view of the permanent way department, however, they suffered from very unequal weight distribution – 12.0 tonnes on the leading axles, 13.9 tonnes on the front coupled axle and only 8.05 on the second coupled axle. Sadly, moreover, as they became outclassed on express work they were deemed unsuitable for secondary duties and all were withdrawn accordingly between 1873 and 1877.

Between 1867 and 1873 the KFNB also built a class of fifty-two 2-4-0's of Series IVb for mixed traffic use but the culmination of their 2-4-0 building was Series IIb3 (in the fresh class numbering scheme begun in 1881) delivered by St. EG in 1881. In this class of eight the outside cylinders (400×632mm) were placed between the leading wheels and the front coupled axle, which gave improved weight distribution, and outside Stephenson link motion was used which must have been interesting to watch at speed. The driving wheels were 1740mm diameter as they were originally intended for semi-fast work (rather than the best expresses) between Prerau and Mahrisch Ostrau but the day of the express 2-4-0 was over by the time they appeared. After the KFNB became part of the kk St.B in 1908 they were often to be seen on slow passenger trains between Vienna and Brunn (Brno) and Vienna and Marchegg. Four of them passed to the BBO and were scrapped in 1925.

A relatively level road and a marked sympathy with British practice on the KFNB led it to show revived interest in the use of singles when all other Austrian railways were equipping themselves with four coupled passenger locomotives. After having ordered only coupled engines for over fifteen years in 1862 the KFNB commissioned Sigl to build a class of five very neat outside cylindered outside framed 2-2-2's with 395×632mm cylinders and 1976mm driving wheels for the light expresses – perhaps 50 tonnes behind the tender – from Vienna to Marchegg and Vienna to Brunn (Brno). Nine years later four further 2-2-2's of a somewhat similar but far from identical design were ordered from Stroussberg of Hannover. The cylinders were 13mm less in the bore but the same stroke, the driving wheels were reduced to 1962mm and the trailing axle was under the firebox. Whereas, however, the 1862 series had only weatherboards turned over at the top the 1871 engines had roomy cabs with side-windows. A further four 2-2-2's came from Floridsdorf the next year, dimensionally very close to – and in the case of wheels and cylinders the same as – those of the year before but, again, not identical. The Floridsdorf engines worked largely in territory that is now Polish. They remained as built until scrapped in the first five years of this century. The earlier Sigl series and the Floridsdorf four underwent drastic rebuilds at Floridsdorf in 1882/83 emerging as 2-4-0's, the last of which ran until 1913. Amongst the regular duties undertaken by the eight newer 2-2-2's was the hauling of the 60 tonne "Kurierzuge" from Vienna to Brunn (143km) in 2 hours 12 minutes running time.

The optimism of the late sixties and early seventies which had expressed itself in the great public works in Vienna and in the great upsurge in railway building and had culminated in the Vienna Exhibition of 1873 led to the setting up of too many speculative enterprises and to an overstretching of the national resources which, in turn, brought about the financial crash on the Vienna Stock Exchange in the Summer of 1873 and a subsequent recession in trade. Many of the railways promoted in the preceding five years and then in course of building found themselves with the greatest difficulty in calling upon capital and railways already completed and in operation were beset by traffic shrinkage and the general shortage of money. Furthermore railways, such as the Arlbergbahn, for which there was considerable public demand, were found to be incapable of being financed at all by private capital and it was not, therefore, until the Austrian Government resumed its role as an owner and operator of railways in the eighties that the Arlbergbahn came into existence. Whilst it stayed in the discussion stage the Vorarlbergbahn, in the extreme West of Austria remained in maidenly isolation from other Austrian lines from the date of its opening in July 1872 until the Arlberg route became operational in 1884, worked by ten demure locomotives supplied by Krauss of Munich in 1871 and 72, six short wheelbase 2-4-0's and a matching foursome of 0-6-0's designed to have as many parts as possible in common.

This unpropitious year of 1873 which had been intended – by the Vienna International Exhibition – to mark a high point in the national achievments of Austria became a punctuation point in its locomotive history. No longer were railways promoted in all directions in the belief that a railway had only to be constructed to prove a source of reward to its promoters. Instead every capital proposal had to be capable of withstanding very critical and sceptical inspection and the operation of existing railways became subject to a campaign for economy. Only in the late seventies did this situation ease substantially and there was a marked thaw in the eighties.

Changes had come about in the locomotive building scene in the sixties and seventies, however, irrespective of these events. In 1867 Georg Sigl acquired the works of Wenzel Guenther in Wiener Neustadt, carrying on, besides locomotive building, the making of oil presses, ships engines, water works machinery, armaments and conveyors. The lift in the Votivkirche in Vienna, for instance, was made at Wiener Neustadt. In 1875 the locomotive business was hived off as a separate limited company, as will be referred to again in the course of the next few pages.

The Guenther works had been much strengthened in 1858 by the arrival of Josef Hall, previously the technical director of Maffei, at Munich, to take charge of the works. Hall (c. 1810 to 1870) was the arch champion of the outside framed outside cylindered locomotive which he had made a thoroughly practical proposition by his own design of crank pins and outside eccentrics to suit outside Stephenson valve gear thus making it easier to abolish the inside motion with which other designs of outside framed locomotives were frequently equipped allowing the overhang on them to be reduced by moving the cylinders rearward. The outside frames also made it possible, by allowing the boiler to drop lower in the frames, to use a larger diameter boiler (and, thus, to have the same heating surface with less length) without raising the centre of gravity – considered very important at that period – whilst at the same time enabling the springs to be moved to the ends of the axles and decreasing the tendency to roll. The Hall type 0-6-0 or 0-8-0 became a mainstay of Austrian locomotive practice for some three decades, though not to the exclusion of inside frames or inside valve gears.

The two main lines which reached Vienna in the three years before the recession – the Kaiser Franz Joseph Bahn and the Osterreichische Nord West Bahn – were essentially railways of Bohemia and, in the latter case, Moravia which had penetrated a short distance into the heartland of Austria in order to enter the capital. A parallel comment, of course, may equally be made of the KFNB of whose mileage not much over 11% fell into post – 1918 Austria though in locomotive affairs the KFNB originated national trends where its newer neighbours were essentially followers of established patterns. The Franz Josef Bahn had only sixteen years of independence (from 1868 to its absorption by the state in May 1884) during which it was worked by two classes of 2-4-0, fifty four engines in all which, together with fifty six 0-6-0 tender engines sufficed for its needs through the lean years. All these were outside framed outside cylindered locomotives of "Hall" type. Twenty three of the 0-6-0's which were given the Series number 35 on the kk St. B survived to become BBO property and the last one was in service until 1929. In 1879/80 a class of thirteen 4-4-0's was put to work and immediately prior to the line's passing into state control a class of ten Hall type 0-8-0's was built but these passed to the Czech railways with the Bohemian lines in 1918. The 0-8-0's were long lived and examples were still working in the fifties.

It is more difficult to discuss the ONWB, of which the earliest section (Josefstadt to Turnau or Jaromer to Turnau) was opened in 1858, since only a minute portion of its route to Vienna (finally opened in 1872) remained Austrian after 1918. The ONWB was an early user of the 4-4-0 type, including some examples with extraordinarily short wheelbase and some subsequent examples of this type from Class 15 (dating from 1883 to 1887) survived to serve the BBO until 1925 though the bulk of the locomotives which came into BBO hands were 2-6-0's (360's and 460's) dating from this century. ONWB locomotives of the early seventies were characteristically Wiener Neustadt products, outside framed and outside cylindered, the 4-4-0's having outside motion in addition but in 1872 the railway switched its affections by ordering its first 0-8-0 from Floridsdorf with inside frame though still with outside cylinders and motion, subsequently increasing its stock of these to fifty four.

The 0-8-0 was likewise well represented on the Sudbahn with Classes 33, 34 and 35a, b and c. The twenty six engines of Class 33 dating from 1853/54 and rebuilds of Engerth types had remarkable lives – three of them being still in service on the BBO in 1927. Class 34 (1867) was the first with eight coupled wheels to use Hall patent crank pins and came from St. EG – not, as one might have expected, from Maffei or Wiener Neustadt – for use over the Brenner pass. The 35a's of 1871/72 survived to become BBO class 471 and did not finally disappear until 1932 but the 35b and c's, though even longer lived, went to Yugoslavia and Italy along with the Sudbahn lines there. The true maid-of-all work on the Sudbahn as on most British railways was, however the 0-6-0 and it outnumbered the 0-8-0's by a very substantial margin. Even so about ten per cent of the Sudbahn locomotive stock consisted of 0-8-0's, a reflection both of the mountainous areas it served and of its pre-eminence as a national and international freight hauler. It is interesting to do a dimensional comparison of the Brenner 0-8-0's of 1867 (Sudbahn Class 34) with the basically similar but inside framed contemporaries on the St. EG (Class 42, also dating from 1867). Both came from the same works. The table below shows these comparisons; with the dimensions of the kk St. B Class 73 of 1885 added for comparison.

	Sudbahn 34	St. EG 42	kk St. B 73
Cylinders' diameter	500mm	470mm	500mm
stroke	610mm	632mm	570mm
Driving wheels	1070mm	1186mm	1120mm
Boiler pressure	9 Atm	9 Atm	11 Atm
Grate area	1.84m^2	1.90m^2	2.25m^2
Heating surface	183.20m^2	180.40m^2	182.00m^2
Gross weight	47300kg	44350kg	55000kg

A significant change to be noted in the 1885 dimensions is the upping of the pressure to 11 atmospheres made possible largely by the introduction of steel into boiler making in the seventies.

For passenger traffic in the seventies the Sudbahn, long a user of the four wheeled leading truck – from the days of the Norris type locomotives – turned to the 4-4-0 type. Probably the most interesting development was the locomotive "Rittinger" which was exhibited by the Wiener Neustadt works at the Vienna Universal Exhibition in 1873, a large wheeled (1900mm) 4-4-0 with the trailing axle behind the firebox, outside frames, cylinders and motion, of Hall type, the boiler pressed to 10 atmospheres and the cylinders 411mm×632mm. The actual exhibition engine was bought by the ONWB but a sister was bought by the Sudbahn (where it carried the running number 201) and delighted its purchaser by hauling a 20 coach (160 tonne) train up a 3.6% grade at 45km/h. On the ONWB Elbel developed this theme the following year by ordering from Floridsdorf two further 4-4-0 in which he asked for increased grate area (from $1.64m^2$ to $1.80m^2$) and heating surface ($107.60m^2$ to $111.00m^2$) but with the line of the cylinders (410×632mm) brought back to near the centre of the boiler barrel and the rear axle the driven axle. He also had the bogie wheelbase increased from 1320mm to 1800mm. Moreover he fitted a cab of more generous proportions. Moving the cylinders was a retrograde step and they soon reverted to the original position but the basic form of the modified "Rittinger" design was adopted by the Austrian main line railways as the type for express work through the remainder of the seventies and eighties, except on the St. EG where, as has been narrated earlier, the French type 2-4-2 prevailed, doubtless as a consequence of the French capital invested in the company. The Kronprinz Rudolf Bahn ordered 4-4-0 locomotives from Wiener Neustadt in 1877, the KFJB from the same builder in 1879/80, the KFNB in 1884 using 2002mm driving wheels, probably the largest used on an Austrian four coupler up to that time.

The Sudbahn, with which this discussion began, ordered the Class 17a's from Floridsdorf, in 1882, with, out of deference to the profile of the road on which they were to run, only 1720mm driving wheels, soon to be folowed by the 17b's (1884) and the 17c's (1885). The principal expresses taken on by the Sudbahn from Bavaria over the lines of the old Tiroler Staatsbahn and thence to Innsbruck and over the Brenner to Italy and the expresses from Vienna Sudbahnhof southward to Graz or through Bruck a.d. Mur to Leoben were handled by 17b's and c's, later fitted with vacuum ejectors and mufflers on the cab roof.

Despite its early use of 0-8-0 engines the Sudbahn was, as remarked, a large user of 0-6-0's. The eleven locos of the 32a class built by Floridsdorf in 1874 for the Vienna, Pottendorf and Wiener Neustadt line (which was worked from the outset by the Sudbahn), though short wheel based, long boiler engines were notable engines for their time but are overshadowed in interest by the 24 class, delivered in 1872 by St. EG for the GKB, the working of which also reposed in Sudbahn hands. With smaller cylinders and wheels than the 32a's and not much more than three quarters the total weight of the latter they were important in two respects. Firstly, so far as the Sudbahn were concerned they were the first locomotives to have a boiler pressure of 10 atmospheres or more and secondly they broke the spell of the long-boiler locomotives by using a shorter higher pitched boiler with the firebox above the rear axle and a grate area of $2.00m^2$ compared with only $1.7m^2$ on the 32a's.

As a result in part of the 1873 financial crisis and in part of a growing public concern over the conditions of labour in factories and mines, particularly in the industrial areas of Moravia and in the mines of Galicia the doctrine of *laissez faire* which had been all but supreme in economic matters since the first half of the fifties began to give way to an attitude more closely resembling the modern Social Democratic approach. Parties in the Reichsrath were divided, however, on racial, territorial and religious lines as much as on political stance and it would be deceiving to represent this on a party political basis in the modern sense. In 1877 when the mainly German Liberal Party was the dominant force in the government an Act was passed permitting government acquisition of private railways and at the end of the seventies, in response to the pressure from manufacturing industry for tariff protection amended duties were introduced giving such protection in a substantial degree. In 1879 the Liberals lost sway to a multi-party coalition, mainly non-German, under Count Taaffe to whose lot fell the actual commencement of state railway ownership. Taaffe's government was destined to rule for the next fourteen years. It introduced (1884 and 1885), and enforced, laws relating to the regulation of work in factories and mines and the employment of children and women followed by further Acts covering compulsory insurance against accidents and sickness, the legislation being modelled upon German practice.

The Austrian government, in fact, resumed the ownership of railways in 1880 as the kk St. B (kaiserlich-konigliche Österreichische Staatsbahnen – Imperial and Royal Austrian State Railways), taking over the working of the KRB from the 1st January 1880 and the KEB from January, 1882 with full ownership from the Summer of 1884, at which date also the KFJB, the NOSWB and a number of lines outside the frontiers of modern Austria joined the fold. The significance of 1884 is that in that year the Arlbergbahn was opened, promoted by the state from the outset so that once it was operational the state controlled the whole of the western mainline from Vienna Westbahnhof through to the Swiss frontier though the smaller Vorarlbergerbahn on the extreme west of Austria, state worked from 1882, did not become state owned until 1885.

For freight working through the Arlberg tunnel, the west approach to which was particularly severe – twenty five kilometres of a ruling grade of 3.1% with curves as little as 200 metre radius, the newly formed kk St. B administration in Vienna invited designs from three leading builders, Wiener Neustadt, Floridsdorf and Krauss, Munich, to be capable of handling 175 tonne loads at a minimum of 12km/hr over 2.6% grades. Four locomotives were ordered from the first of these builders and two and five respectively from the other two. The Wiener Neustadt design was a large but straightforward Hall-type 0-8-0 with 540×610mm cylinders, 1140mm wheels, a pressure of 11 Atmospheres and a grate area of 2.46m². Like the Sudbahn 24 class they had the horizontal centre line of the boiler raised sufficiently so that the firebox was over the rear axle. The Floridsdorf design was dimensionally similar but a tank locomotive with inside frames to the front three coupled axles and outside frames to the rear pair and under the cab, bunker and rear water tank. The Krauss offering were 0-8-0 side tank engines in which the cylinder diameter was 500mm (compared with 540 in the Wiener Neustadt locomotive and 550 in the Floridsdorfers) and the pressure was down to 10 Atmospheres. These were the least successful of the three designs. Examples of the other two lasted till the electrification but the Krauss locomotives did not.

For passenger trains over the Arlberg the kk St. B ordered from Krauss in Munich the class of five 2-6-0's originally titled AIV, later Class 9 and later still 28. In many ways these locomotives, of markedly Bavarian characteristics, were pointers to the future of Austrian policy. In them, for the first time on an Austrian locomotive, the Helmholtz two wheeled leading truck and the 2-6-0 arrangement were used. The valve gear was the Heusinger von

Waldegg type (in all essentials Walschaert). The profile of the locomotives was essentially modern and pointed, in all but one particular namely the fact that they were simples rather than compounds, to the direction which kk St. B locomotive policy would be taking in the next three decades.

Compounding, in the spreading of which under Karl Gölsdorf's direction, the kk St. B was destined to play such a prominent part, owed its introduction to Austria to the KFNB, whose Locomotive Superintendent, W. Rayl, in 1879 rebuilt an old 2-4-0 "Nagy Maros" taken over from the kk Sudostlichen Staatsbahn and dating from 1847, as a compound on Mallet's principles. Like many such experiments undertaken with limited commitment it seems to have failed to give satisfactory results. Nor did the St. EG appear to be much better pleased with a Webb 2-2-2-0 named, for a reason not now apparent, "Combermere", supplied in 1884 by Sharp Roberts & Co. Though this survived until 1896 its last years were not, it would seem, very active though about 1890 it had the distinction of being used to obtain information on receiver pressures for Gölsdorf's first compound designs.

Compounding was seen as a very pressing matter in most of Central Europe where deep mined coal was scarce and, relatively, expensive so that locomotives frequently had to make do with surface mined brown coal. In Austria additional point was given to these considerations by the fact that improved conditions of work in mines had tended to increase the cost of production whilst the introduction of tariffs impeded the import of non-Austrian coal or, as the reverse of the coin, made it dearer. The building and operating of compound locomotives is, however, the theme of the next chapter and is best considered there.

The imposition of tariffs upon imported machinery gave impetus to the development of locomotive building in the Austrian Empire. Krauss of Munich who had designs on a greater share of the market for locomotives created by the expansion of Austrian railway mileage in the seventies solved the tariff problem by building a daughter works at Linz in Lower Austria, completed in 1880. Krauss had made a name for locomotives for light railways and narrow gauges both for public and industrial lines but after opening the Linz Works catered increasingly for main line locomotives.

George Sigl who had, though not himself a dedicated locomotive man, played an important part in establishing the native building of locomotives withdrew from the Wiener Neustadt Locomotive Works in 1875 to devote himself to general engineering, which he did almost to the time of his death in 1887. The works, under the new limited company was very active until the dismemberment of Austria after 1918 and succumbed, finally, to the combination of the slump and the fearsome financial problems of post 1918 Austria. Haswell severed his long-standing association with the St. EG works in 1882, having outlasted his old antagonist, Wilhelm Engerth, by two years.

Floridsdorf Works (actually situated in Gross Jedlersdorf) under the direction of the celebrated Bernhard Demmer flourished throughout the seventies and eighties. Founded by the Wiener Bankverein in partnership with Ludwig Becker of the KFNB and Karl Hornbostel of the KEB and incorporated in September 1869 the company scarcely looked back. Building of the works began in April 1870 and the first locomotive was delivered in July 1871 – the hundredth came out only two years later.

Whilst the prosperity of Floridsdorf was thus being founded the Works at Mödling, a few miles South of Vienna was set up in 1872, employing as its chief executive F. X. Mannhard, for many years with George Sigl in his Vienna works. The first locomotive completed was an outside framed Hall-type 2-4-0 for the KRB delivered in 1873 but after 32 locomotives had been delivered the financial crisis of 1873 and the subsequent depression forced the works to close in 1874.

The developing interest in continuous brakes, which in England culminated in the Newark brake trials, led the Sudbahn to experiment with the Smith vacuum brake in 1877. The Sudbahn had perhaps the most mountainous terrain to contend with of any of the Austrian railways and had accordingly the most pressing interest in continuous and preferably automatic brakes. The superintendant of its repair shops in Vienna was John Hardy (1820–1896) a Newcastle man and former apprentice at Robert Stephenson's Forth Street works. From 1846–1860 he had been in charge of the workshop of the Chemin de Fer de l'Ouest at Rouen and from 1860–1884 in a similar position with the Sudbahn in Vienna. John Hardy used the experience of working and maintaining the Smith brake to introduce his own improvements in the mechanism and design and became Austria's pre-eminent brake expert being closely involved in the introduction of the automatic vacuum brake. The firm of Gebrüder Hardy of Vienna, run by his sons, supplied vacuum braking equipment to the Continent. Hardy's patents were developed in this country by the Vacuum Brake Co. Ltd. but it was not until 1895 (the province of the next chapter) that the automatic vacuum was adopted by the kk St. B and the KFNB. The St. EG, by contrast, and perhaps because of its French connections favoured the Westinghouse system.

During the period covered by this chapter only very limited use was made by Austrian railways of tank locomotives (which by one of the perversities of language are called "Tenderlokomotiven" in German). The Engerth locomotives which properly fall into this class were the most numerous group and have already been noticed as have the tank locomotives built for the Arlbergbahn. These apart one of the more interesting of tank classes was the group of 0-6-0 tanks supplied to the KPRB by Krauss of Munich and the Swiss Locomotive Works, Winterthur – the latter a very uncommon supplier of locomotives to Austria – in 1872/4. These survived to come into the hands of BBÖ as Class 62 and one was in service until 1929. Fitted with Heusinger (Walschaert) valve gear they were probably the first locomotives in Austria to be so fitted and almost certainly the first tank locomotives.

The KRB scored another first with these locomotives when No. 76, one of the Krauss-built examples (Works No. 193 of 1872) was fitted with an electric headlight – on the arc principle – powered by a generator and small high speed reciprocating steam engine placed immediately behind the chimney.

The Kremstalbahn which owned the line running due South from the KEB at Linz through the Krems valley to Steyrling and Bad Hall and for which the firm of Krauss had supplied much of the capital had a locomotive stud of ten – three 0-4-0's, four 2-4-0's and three 0-6-0's – all supplied, not surprisingly, by Krauss from their Linz Works. The 2-4-0's, which were dated between 1892 and 1899 closely resembled the tanks supplied by their makers for branch line work on the Bavarian Railways and were notable for the extremely wide spacing of the axle centres.

The working of the single station coal branch from Zeltweg to Fohnsdorf was taken over by KRB from the mine owners, the Vordenberger Erzverein, who worked the Eisenerz open iron stone quarry. With it they acquired a 0-4-0 outside cylinder side tank built by F. Wöhlert (Works No. 316) of Berlin, the solitary example of the work of this maker falling within our scope.

Other tank classes built new in Austria before 1890 included the St. EG Class IVa, dating from 1870, a long boilered outside cylindered saddletank design in which Haswell used his patented Wellblech corrugated firebox. These were built for lightly laid branches and the total weight was only 27300kg. With a working pressure of 10 Atmospheres they were in advance of small locomotive practice at the time, though the cylinder dimensions (281×432mm) were about average for the type. Certainly the Class 41 0-8-0 tanks – carrying a combination of side and pannier tanks – built ten years later had a working pressure of only 9 Atmospheres, in combination with 450×600mm cylinders. They were, incidentally, the first 0-8-0 tank class in Austria. Haswell, who was, before all else, a practical man, may well have considered that, in a locomotive intended for local freight and yard duties, the advantage of ease of handling conferred by the lower boiler pressure of the Class 41's outweighed the theoretically greater efficiency attainable by the use of higher boiler pressure.

A locomotive development which came from the period of financial stringency of the seventies as a joint brain child of Elbel, of the KFNB and Louis Adolf Gölsdorf (1837–1909) of the Sudbahn was the use of small and light tank locomotives carrying a baggage or parcel compartment on the same chassis and intended to deal with the problem of working very sparsely trafficked branches with economy. The examples for both railways were built at Floridsdorf, for the KFNB as 0-2-2's and for the Sudbahn as 0-4-2's, in each case with the cylinders under the cab. The former used 225×400mm cylinders and a pressure of 10 Atmospheres but the Sudbahners were more daring using 250×400mm cylinders and 12 Atmospheres, high for 1879, the year in which they appeared. Ten years later the Sudbahn returned to the theme with a class of light 2-2-0 tanks without the baggage compartment and in another period of financial stringency (the mid-thirties) the idea was resurrected again. The immediate result in Austria, however was a development during the 1890's of an interest in self-contained steam railcars, to be considered in Chapter III.

The seventies and eighties were a period of rebuilding of existing locomotive types which had become outmoded before being worn out and in a number of cases, such as the KFNB goods 2-4-0's (later kk St. B Class 289) dating from 1849–53, conversion to tank engines. Thirty-three of these engines were rebuilt by the KFNB in its own shops at Floridsdorf between 1868 and 1882 as saddletanks for shunting duties and one of them (the "Licaon") survives on exhibition on a pedestal outside the divisional headquarters of OBB at Linz. In general, however, shunting was undertaken by elderly tender-locomotives and the contrary practice of the KFNB in this respect is yet another reflection of its affinity for British practices.

The eighties closed with the railways poised for important developments – compounding, higher permitted axle loads, continuous automatic brakes with the concomitant of higher train speeds, the beginning of superheating. By the nineties Austria was politically more settled, the financial situation was much improved and the state railway administration was settled into control. The new decade opened a new era.

Chapter IV
Mainly about compounds

The ebullience of the early seventies never returned to the Austrian railway scene but, as has been noted in the previous chapter, the eighties saw a steady rebuilding of confidence which, in the nineties provided the basis of a series of developments in railways and locomotives which placed Austria for a decade and a half in the front ranks of technical innovators. The nineties, both in national life and in the narrower confines of railway affairs, had about them a stability and a bedrock of real achievement which causes many contemporary Austrians to look back on them as a kind of golden age.

So far as the structure of the system was concerned the opening of the Arlbergbahn, completing through East to West communication from Russia to Switzerland wholly over Austrian territory was the most notable event and its completion in the face of financial uncertainty and the sheer vastness of its civil engineering problems led, by a natural progression, to demands for a Tauern line, again involving very heavy engineering and tunnels on a massive scale to provide the missing North-South link to join Salzburg with Klagenfurt.

A strengthening programme in the eighties and nineties removed the more onerous restrictions on axle loadings – though Austrian permitted loads remained low by comparison with Great Britain – whilst the track itself was improved, inter alia, by the use of steel rails, by improved ballasting and by re-alignment of curves and junctions. Signals and telegraphs were also the subject of development. In the locomotive department the introduction of steel, bringing with it the benefit of the opportunity to increase the working pressure of boilers without putting up the weight, produced a marked increase in power output per ton. The possibility of using steel in the production of reliable cranked axles, items so long looked at askance in Austrian locomotive building circles, revived interest in the use of inside cylinders, laid aside after early misadventures on the KFNB in the thirties and forties and hardly looked at thereafter. Furthermore the introduction of continuous brakes had made possible improvements in train times by decreasing stopping distances and thereby allowing the use of higher speeds between the more closely spaced stops or speed checks.

Two further constituents of change were in the discussion and experimental stages namely the search for drier and hotter steam and the use of two stage expansion – compounding. Consideration of these two factors was not limited to Austria but Austria produced one additional factor peculiar to itself namely the arrival upon the scene of Dr Karl Gölsdorf (1861–1916), a fitting candidate for inclusion in the select gallery of outstanding locomotive engineers, both as an inventor in his own right and as a recognizer and developer of sound principles first expounded by others, a combination not dissimilar to that which two generations before had made Haswell a great – though in general personal characteristics they could hardly have been less alike. Though he brought to bear upon the problems of Austrian locomotive development some of the detachment of the academic his background was, in fact, firmly rooted in railway life. His father was Louis Gölsdorf, locomotive superintendant of the Sudbahn from 1885 to 1908 and he thus grew up in a Viennese household where the operation and maintenance of locomotives was the acceptable topic of conversation among the men.

During his college days in Vienna he put in a great deal of time in his father's office and after leaving college he spent seven years in the St. EG works. In 1891 he was taken into the chief mechanical engineer's office of the kk St. B and shortly afterwards, recognising his extraordinary talents, the Chief Mechanical Engineer, H. Kargl, allowed Gölsdorf a free hand in creating the locomotive stock required for working the rapidly growing (both in route mileage and traffic) kk St. B system. Gölsdorf succeeded Kargl as head of the department in 1906. During his twenty years of office he produced 25 basic locomotive designs with variations and sub-classes introducing such later innovations as superheating and piston valves. Disregarding trifling deviations the total number of classes and sub-classes was forty-seven.

It will have been noted already that the pattern of nineteenth century locomotive building in Austria differed from that on British home railways. It was virtually unknown (except in the case of St. EG which organised its works as a locomotive manufactory and built as a contractor for other administrations) for railways to build the locomotives they used. The exceptions to contractor-built locomotives hardly use up the fingers of two hands, the most notable being six 2-4-0 passenger locomotives built by the Kaiserin Elizabeth Bahn in 1863 and a trio of 0-6-0 tender engines in 1866. Design accordingly rested much more with the contractor than with the railway. An important customer such as the Sudbahn would undoubtedly issue stringent specifications and outlines of requirements and would dictate which changes of practice, if any, were to be incorporated. At the other end of the scale a small railway such as the Kremstalbahn or the Muhlkreisbahn would rely necessarily almost entirely upon what the contractor could offer.

Gölsdorf Senior was much more of a supervisor or overseer of new designs and much less an originator of design than one of his British counterparts. The entry of his son into the locomotive department of the state railways in 1891 changed the balance radically. Until that time the KFNB (and the KEB up to the time of the absorption into the state system) alone had maintained a system at all like that prevailing in Britain.

From the time of the appointment of the younger Gölsdorf in 1891 it became clear that henceforth it was to be in his hands that both the principles and details of design were to rest, though his openminded and generous outlook caused his yoke to ride so easily that the team he controlled – both contractors and his own subordinates – soon became loyal admirers and adherents.

So far as express work was concerned interest in compounding ran neck and neck on the KFNB under W. Rayl and the kk St. B under Kargl and Gölsdorf. In goods locomotive design, however, the former was a little ahead. In 1889 he designed a class of twenty-four 0-6-0 tender locomotives (later kk St. B Class 159) built by Wiener Neustadt in which the cylinders were 480 and 740mm diameter × 660mm stroke, wheels 1440mm diameter and the pressure 12 Atmospheres. Being of the long-boiler arrangement, they had a coupled wheelbase of only 3.50m. The grate area was 2.20 square metres and the heating surface 133.5 square metres. Besides economy in fuel and water, which Rayl had expected, he found that the handling and working characteristics were improved. The softer blast dealt kindly with the fire bed lifting less of the inferior fuel and thus leaving the smokebox cleaner and decreasing lineside fire risks. In these locomotives Rayl used the von Borries' system of compounding.

Cautiously Rayl contented himself with his compound goods classes for some years, following his 0-6-0's in 1894 with a class of 2-6-0's, eventually totalling twenty-one, built, again, by Wiener Neustadt, using the same dimension for cylinders and driving wheels and a boiler with the same grate area but longer in the barrel and smokebox so that the heating surface was 147.50 square metres compared with 133.5 square metres in the earlier design. Althouth the total weight was increased from 42,000kg to 51,000kg the adhesive weight actually went down to 38,600kg so that the weight distribution was very even. Fitted with double domes, the leading dome carrying the safety valves, and a sand box between and carrying a stove-pipe chimney they were a most handsome design and, if anything, were improved in looks when the leading dome with its spring balances was abolished and pop safety valves were fitted on the rear dome. A prominent feature was the outside exhaust pipe from the low pressure (off-side) cylinder to the smokebox.

Nevertheless he remained unwilling to commit his crack express workings – Vienna Nord to Cracow – to compounds and as the weight of the trains, coupled with the additional demands on steam created by continuous brakes and train heating, was outrunning the powers of the existing 4-4-0's he produced an entirely new design, to a wheel arrangement (4-4-2) fresh to Austria and Europe. The date of the design was 1893 and they were still in production when the KFNB was merged with the state railways in 1909 by which year a total of fifty-seven were in service. The limiting factor in the design was the 14 tonne top weight per axle imposed by the Permanent Way Department.

To achieve the desired power output (700/800 horsepower) Rayl used the highest boiler pressure employed on an Austrian locomotive up to that time – 13 Atmospheres – and provided a firebox with 2.9 square metres of grate area placed between the rear coupled wheels and over the trailing truck, raising the total heating surface to 152 square metres. The driving wheels were 1960mm, the two outside cylinders 470×600mm. Heusinger valve gear was used, together with outside frames, an ample two window cab, double domes and a sand-box between. On test one reached 125km/hr (78m.p.h.).

These handsome and innovative locomotives were soon to be overshadowed by the virtuoso performances in locomotive design from the hand of Gölsdorf and, indeed, have never received the notice which, it seems to the author, they deserve. They were divided between Wien Nord, Lundenburg, Prerau and Cracow depots but thirty came into the hands of BBO after 1918 where, being in the unfortunate position of a non-standard minority on a railway basically over provided with locomotives, they lasted intact only until 1927 being thereafter withdrawn as they fell due for general repairs, the last two, however, surviving just long enough to receive the DR numbers 14001 and 002 after the Anschluss.

About the time that Rayl was designing his elegant Atlantics Gölsdorf's design team was completing the drawings for his Class 59 0-6-0 tender locomotives, built by Wiener Neustadt, beginning in 1893. In this, as in Rayl's 0-6-0's, two cylinders were used, but in it was incorporated his own design of starting valve which by its simplicity and utility, made him a modest fame through much of Europe and, to a limited extent, America. Because the wheel diameter was only 1300mm against 1400mm in Rayl's design of 1889 he was able to bring the coupled wheelbase down to 3160mm (again 3500mm in Rayl's engines). Other statistics were: cylinders 500 and 740mm×632mm stroke, pressure 12 Atmospheres, grate area 1.80 square metres, heating surface 134 square metres. The weight was 42600kg against Rayl's 42000.

It was probably because of the difficulty in balancing exactly the thrust of the high and low pressure pistons at every speed but more specifically at high speeds that Rayl had shrunk from employing compounding on his express locomotives. Experiments in Germany by von

Borries and his associates are said to have suggested that divergencies of up to 15% between the two cylinders were insufficient to affect the performance of the locomotive adversely, but the author has been unable to locate a published report of such experiments nor it it possible to see to what control the locomotive under test could be compared, much less the criteria of comparison. Whether emboldened by these experiments or determined to find the outcome by actual experience Gölsdorf set in hand the designing of his celebrated Class 6 inside framed compound 4-4-0's. His leading bogie had the very long wheelbase of 2700mm, only a hundred less than the coupled wheelbase. The boiler was pitched high so that the firebox came between the coupled axles and the springing and compensating gear was all under the axles. The designer used the freedom given by this high pitching of the boiler to give it a grate area of 2.90 square metres, as much as Rayl had managed with a rear trailing axle to carry it and, at the same time, he achieved a total heating surface of 155 square metres, 3 square metres more than in the Atlantics. For the first time he used the famous Gölsdorf twin domes coupled by an external pipe carrying the safety valves.

The Class 6's were an outstanding success, producing a power output equivalent to Rayl's Atlantics with a total weight of 56,600kg compared with 60,000kg in the Atlantics. Their capabilities, in fact, exceeded the ability of the lines on which they ran to receive them or at least to allow full rein to their potential.

Following the success of Rayl's compound 2-6-0's Gölsdorf set about designing a corresponding type (the Class 60's) incorporating the features which had helped to make the Class 6's so outstanding, notably the high pitched boiler and large grate area, 13 Atmospheres pressure and, of course his starting valve. The diameter of the high pressure cylinder was increased to 520mm, the low pressure remaining at 740mm but the stroke decreased from 680 to 632mm. The driving wheel diameter was 1,300mm (against 1,440mm in Rayl's 2-6-0's). This class was built at Floridsdorf in 1894/5 and was quickly followed by the celebrated 2-6-2 tanks for working the Vienna Stadtbahn.

The Stadtbahn in Vienna is a near analog of the Inner Circle in London with the disadvantage that the circle is not closed. There is a break between Gumpendorfer-Strasse and Margarethengurtel which prevents circular running. This apart the route, which follows the line of the old outer fortifications of Vienna and encircles the so-called suburbs, the former "villages" between the inner fortifications (now the site of the Ring) and the outer fortifications (now the Gurtel) was a difficult proposition to work by steam. Stations are close together and because the line is partly in tunnel and partly on viaduct there are numerous short sharp climbs and descents. Moreover, following as it does a path through densely built-up areas the line, in steam days, was an especial target for criticism on grounds of smoke emission, always a problem to Austrian designers, bearing in mind the types of coal at their disposal.

The class which Gölsdorf produced for these duties in 1895, entrusting the building again to Floridsdorf, was a 2–6–2 T version of the Class 60's, modified in that instead of the large fire grate area for inferior coal there was a much smaller one (2.30 square metres) to suit oil burning on Holden's system, then in full cry on the Great Eastern Railway. These tanks were given the designation Class 30. A change they shared with the 60's was the final abandonment of spring balances in favour of Coale's type pop safety valves.

The old 0-6-0's of the Sudbahn which worked the bulk of the trains over the Semmering and Brenner passes were able to cope with train weights of the order of 110 to 120 tonnes. By the mid nineties the passenger train weights over these passes had pushed past these limits, necessitating an altogether more powerful locomotive. The Sudbahn never fell wholly under the spell of compounding but in other respects it was willing to accept the precepts of the able young man running the kk St. B locomotive affairs – particularly, no doubt, in view of his paternal connections with the railway. To this demand for increased power the answer propounded was a small wheeled two cylinder simple 4-6-0, a wheel arrangement not used before in Austria. These class 32f 4-6-0's, produced by St. EG in 1896, were a thoroughly Gölsdorf design in everything but the fact of being simple expansion, with 500×680mm cylinders, 1540mm driving wheels, 13 Atmospheres pressure, 2.85 square metres of grate and 184 square metres of heating surface all achieved within a weight of 60,000kg. Only in its use of twin spring balance safety valves did the design lag behind kk St. B practice.

The ONWB also built a 4-6-0 class in 1896, compound with 1650mm driving wheels, which, like the Sudbahn locomotives, came from St. EG. Eventually numbering twenty-four in all it worked outside the limits of modern Austria, based on Nimburg and Reichenberg, and no examples came into BBO stock so that we must pass over them here.

Useful though the Sudbahn Class 32f was on mountain duties it did not suggest a solution to the problems of working the Arlbergbahn which were such as to call for both greater power and increased adhesion. Since the permitted maximum loadings (of the order of 14,150kg) could not be increased the only solution was to increase the number of coupled axles whilst, at the same time, reducing wheel diameter. The result from Gölsdorf's office was the 170 Class which eventually reached a total of 796 locomotives by 1917 plus a further 100 of the superheated version, designated 270, designed initially to lift the heavy summer expresses, sometimes totalling 220 tonnes behind the tender, over the Arlberg but ultimately used widely in Bohemia and Moravia as well. Of these 228 came into the hands of BBO and the last was not withdrawn until 1956. In almost every line the 170's were redolent of Gölsdorf's principles of design – two cylinder compound (540 and 800×632), a boiler pressure of 13 Atmospheres, high pitched boiler with a large grate (3.37 square metres later increased to 3.87) and plenty of heating surface (250 square metres), twin domes, coupled externally, pop safety valves, drive to the third coupled axle and flexibility provided by side play in the axle boxes. The driving wheels were only 1,300mm in diameter and the leading axle was of the Adams type.

The success of the 170's can be described as nothing short of spectacular. Gölsdorf Senior soon adopted it on the Sudbahn for working over the Brenner.

Compared with the Class 56 0-6-0's of 1888 which it displaced from the Arlberg line it generated treble the horsepower and immediately doubled the permissible train weights, all achieved with a gross weight of only 69,000kg against 42,000kg in the 56's. Their designer commented in his memorable essay on Austrian locomotives that on an hours journey, loaded, between Landeck and Langen the boiler evaporated *10 cubic metres of water*.

The St. EG ever conscious of its French capital and antecedents, opted in 1898 for a three cylinder compound 4-4-0, following, in general principles, the design by E. Sauvage for the Nord in France in 1889 in which the high pressure cylinder was placed between the frames and the two low pressures outside with provision for simpling on starting. This locomotive (St. EG Class 2501, kk St. B 506) remained solitary and consequently shortlived. Presumably its actual performance must have disappointed its designer.

On the kk St. B, however the compound 4-4-0 design of Class 6 was developed still further in the 106's. Dimensionally the changes were minor (an increase in the low pressure cylinder diameter from 740 to 760mm and an increase in grate area from 2.90 square metres to 3.10 square metres) though the driving wheel diameter increased from 2120mm to 2140mm yet, because of increased use of steel the weight came *down* from 56,000kg to 55,600kg. As in the case of the 170's the new 106 design was taken up by the senior Gölsdorf for use on the Sudbahn. Forty-two came into BBO ownership and of these seventeen lasted long enough to receive Deutche Reichsbahn numbers.

Though the appearance of the 106's, belonging as it did to Gölsdorf's utilitarian phase, might have been described as homely the Class 9 4-6-0's which came out in 1898 can hardly be described, even euphemistically, as other than exceedingly plain, though marvellous workers. In them the old arrangement of twin domes joined by an external pipe became transmogrified into a massive external pipe (as a steam collector) mounted on two vestigial domes. Outside frames and inside cylinders (530 and 810mm×720mm) were used in conjunction with 1820mm driving wheels and a pressure, for the first time in Austria, of 14 Atmospheres. The grate area at 3.14 square metres was only just in excess of the 106 class 4-4-0's (3.10 square metres) but because of the greater length of the boiler the total heating surface was up from 155.5 square metres in the 106 Class to 207.90 square metres, still not so great as the 250 square metres of the Class 170 2-8-0's but somewhat compensated by the higher pressure. Whereas the 170's produced 1035 drawbar horsepower the Class 9's could turn out 1200 at higher speed. Their stamping ground was the former KRB trans-alpine route, Amstetten, Seltztal, St. Michael and Pontafel, and because they outclassed the Sudbahn 32f's the latter railway also took them up. In moving the cylinders to the inside position Gölsdorf was, no doubt, endeavouring in this express locomotive, to minimise the inherent transverse imbalance induced by the relative sizes of the two cylinder compound arrangement, over riding the long standing Austrian distrust of cranked axles in doing so. In his own case he also had to lay aside briefly his antipathy toward the outside frame so as to achieve the necessary width between the frames to accommodate the cylinders.

His successor and erstwhile assistant, J. Rihosek, rebuilt the Class 9's as simples *c*.1924, using poppet valves, as part of the move away from compounding, discussed more fully in the next chapter, after the formation of the Republic of Austria after the 1914/18 war.

Despite the fact of his numerous patents Gölsdorf was at some pains to emphasise that he was a designer rather than an inventor, a pragmatist rather than an originator and investigator of technical theory. The man who provided the theoretical basis, which Gölsdorf himself never failed to acknowledge, of the impeccable behaviour of Gölsdorf eight and, later, ten coupler locomotives over curved track was R. Helmholtz, chief designer at the Munich Works of Krauss whose design of linked pony truck and advocacy of simple side play in the coupled axles had influenced him in designing the 2-8-0's of Class 170.

The success which these had enjoyed led him on to the production of the ten coupled Class 180 with which he crowned the nineteenth century. Once again he used the two outside cylinder (560 and 850×632mm) compound arrangement with a boiler pressure of 14 Atmospheres, allied to a driving wheel diameter of 1,300mm. The boiler, high pitched as in the 170's with the firebox over the rear coupled wheels, had a grate area of 3.42 square metres and a total heating surface of 203.30 square metres. The third and fourth coupled axles were rigid but the first, second and fifth had side play, allowed for by articulated coupling rods. The drive was onto the fourth axle necessitating a piston rod over 4500mm long, with intermediate support. The by now familiar twin domes, joined externally, the side window cab and the pop safety valves completed the picture. Though the gross weight was up to 66,500kg the axle loading was actually less, averaging 13,300kg.

The initial batch came from Floridsdorf in 1900 but various subsequent batches including a superheated version, in 1909, given the classification 80 and a simple expansion variant (Class 80.90 of 1911) were built elsewhere and production continued until 1922, when a combined total of 274 were taken into the BBO stock, quite apart from numerous examples on ex-Austrian territory and further afield. The Sudbahn, which followed closely on kk St. B practice throughout this period also used 180's.

In 1899 Karl Gölsdorf visited Great Britain where he discovered elements in locomotive building to which he had not previously given much heed but which, he found, struck a chord in him. Though some of his designs up to that time, notably the 6's and 106's, had had visual appeal it was largely the uncontrived result of working out the logic of the design which had produced it, rather than any deliberate attempt to make them eye catchers. Indeed it might have been suggested that the man who had designed the Class 9 4-6-0's could have been rated blind to aesthetic considerations. The visit to Britain, however, awoke in him a hitherto unsuspected propensity for delight in the smooth uncluttered outlines of British locomotives – particularly one may conjecture in Ivatt's Atlantics on the Great Northern and the locomotives of the Great Western, reasserting itself as a great railway under Churchward. Doubtless too he envied British designers the freedom allowed by their seemingly endless supplies of cheap high quality steam coal, a marked contrast to his own situation where only a select few of the top services were allowed clean deep-mined coal, the remainder being fired on a mixture of hard and brown coal, often containing much slack. He must have noted also the lack in Britain of sustained or widespread interest in compounding.

Whether or not his visit had any influence upon his attitude to cranked axles is unlikely ever to be known. Certainly after his return he turned with enthusiasm to the use of this feature of design which he had used only once before, in the Class 9's of 1898. The introduction of high performance steels into locomotive building had undoubtedly removed one of the main Austrian objections to cranked axles but there was perhaps a further and more pressing reason for a change of attitude. The two cylinder asymmetrical compound had reached the extreme limits of size even on the generous width restrictions permitted in Austria. Compounds almost literally could get no bigger with only two cylinders.

The culmination of all these contributing factors was Class 108, Gölsdorf's ultimate in four coupled locomotives, cast in the then fashionable Atlantic mould. Out of a class of 25 only three of the kk St. B examples were based in modern Austria (at Vienna) the rest being divided between Prague, Pilsen and Cracow, but a further eleven were used by the Sudbahn south of the Semmering and came into BBO stock. It may be noted that, for the first time, their designer used four cylinders, the two high pressure of 350mm diameter placed inside and the 600mm diameter low pressures outside, the stroke going up to 680mm. Driving wheel diameter was 2140mm. In them also he used the high running plate, wide opensided splashers and smoothed off profile which, with variations, were to characterise his passenger locomotive designs for the rest of his life.

On the route from Vienna to Prague – 345km of winding main line, crossing three ranges of hills with long stretches of 1% grades – they were able to take along 230 tonne trains at 73km/per hour, achieving a running time only ten minutes behind the modern railcar express on the same route, after making allowance for the frontier stops endured by the latter. No. 108.72 was exhibited at the International Exhibition of rolling stock in Milan in 1906, receiving a Grand Prix award. On a test run it reached a maximum of 143km/hour

(89m.p.h.) but at home it had to submit, officially at least, to the overall restriction of 100km/hour. They were running international expresses south of the Semmering until 1929 but thereafter they were progressively withdrawn, the last being broken up in 1933.

In 1901 the ONWB also put to work its own class of eight Atlantics (later kk St. B Class 208), all worked from Tetschen (now in Czechoslovakia) over which we are obliged to pass for this geographical reason.

The St. EG drawing office, headed by E. Beutel, turned its attention soon afterwards to the same problem of accommodating increased train weights without infringing permanent way restrictions whilst at the same time maintaining and improving train speeds. This time the wheel arrangement selected was the 4-6-0 but again the four cylinder compound arrangement was used as in the 108's but with the important difference that one set of valve gear was provided on each side to serve both high and low pressure cylinders, a practice commendable in theory but complicated to maintain in service. Fourteen were built, all stationed at Vienna East, later becoming kk St. B Class 109, and they were duly taken over by BBO, lasting, like the 108's, till about 1933.

On the kk St. B, however Gölsdorf was taking a somewhat different approach to the same basic problem. On the one hand, because of axle load limitations he was concerned to save weight in every way possible. One of his maxims was "It is hard to save a ton in any one place but instead one can save two pounds each in a thousand places". On the other hand, of course, such weight saving provided problems in adhesion, forcing him to six coupled wheels in situations where, had he had no problems of adhesive weight, he would probably have elected to increase the performance of a four coupled design. Moreover the overall speed restriction of 100km per hour (62.2m.p.h.) enabled him to concentrate more upon vehicular performance in the 80/100km/hour range rather than to concern himself with behaviour at speeds which, officially, were to remain purely theoretical.

These thoughts interested him in the 2-6-2 wheel arrangement, already in use in the United States, as a possible means of improving boiler capacity over the current 4-6-0 practice without increasing the number of axles. The result was the Class 110 2-6-2 of 1905, built at Floridsdorf, in which he again employed the four cylinder compound layout. The six driving wheels, 1820mm diameter as in the St. EG 109's, had a wheelbase of 3.80m, against 4.20m in the 109's and the boiler was lengthened so that the firebox was wholly behind the third coupled axle, free of both the coupled and trailing axles, the latter being at the extreme rear immediately under the footplate. By this means he had virtually unlimited freedom to expand his firebox and took full advantage of it, increasing the grate area to the then unprecedented extent of 4.00 square metres and pushing up the heating surface to 257.85 square metres, still retaining 15 Atmospheres pressure. Mere figures for the latter do not tell the whole story for the proportion of firebox heating surface to total was increased and the evaporative power was correspondingly enhanced and the boiler performance was yet further improved in a superheated version (Class 10) built from 1909 onwards. All this power was contained within a weight of 69,100kg.

On the winding route south-westward through the valley of the Salzach from Salzburg these locomotives used to pour themselves sinuously and, apparently, effortlessly in a way which, to quote Dr Giesl Gieslingen, was "a delight to observe". With their high pitched coned wagon top boiler, extended fireboxes, high running plates and open splashers the class undoubtedly had the authentic greyhound air though their performances so far as speed was concerned were remarkable relative to terrain rather than in the "open" class. The same design, differing only in some of the boiler mountings and the brakes, was built for the Sudbahn and these passed to the Jugoslav State Railways after 1918. Thirty-seven of Class 110 and nineteen of Class 10 were built for the kk St. B distributed between Innsbruck, Villach, Worgl, Salzburg and Vienna N.W. All but two came in the BBO stock and eighteen of Class 10 continued on the ÖBB after 1951.

Because the performance of the 110's and 10's was so outstanding when traffic requirements dictated increased power output on lines where the ruling grades were less than 1% Gölsdorf took what, with hindsight, seems the inevitable step of logic, namely he produced a design in which firstly the wheel diameter was larger and secondly an even larger firebox was carried on four trailing wheels, i.e. a reversed Pacific. The class which resulted was the 210 of 1908 in which he used 2140mm driving wheels and a firebox with 4.60 square metres of grate, the boiler yielding 292.40 square metres of heating surface. Pressure and the general lines of the boiler were unchanged but in the engine work there were changes.

Despite the brilliance of the performance of his 110's and other four cylinder compounds there can be little doubt that Golsdorf received murmurings from the running department about the extra work of maintaining and oiling four sets of valve gear per locomotive where previously they had had two and, moreover, at the difficulty of access to the inside gear. Nor can he have been indifferent to the capital cost of the two further sets of valve gear coming on top of the additional expense of the cranked axle. For these reasons and, doubtless, others, he sacrificed the efficient but expensive arrangements of the 110's for a simpler but, in the event, less efficient, layout in which one valve chest with a single 400mm piston valve controlled admission and exhaust to high and low pressure cylinders on each side. He also altered the diameters of high and low pressure, changing the ratios so that the high pressures were 390mm and the low pressures 660mm in diameter with a 720mm stroke. The 210's were adequate where the 110's had been brilliant. They had suffered possibly from a too hasty period of gestation on the apparently sound but, as it turned out, unfounded assumption that the amendments incorporated did not undermine the basis of the success of the 110's which had formed the starting point of the design. Gölsdorf, disappointed at the results, asked his friend R. Sanzin, the leading contemporary Austrian exponent of the theory of the locomotive, to conduct tests and to make recommendations but despite the making of the amendments which he recommended they never, even in the superheated version (Class 310 of 1911), lived up to the dash of the 110's.

To hand-fire a grate of that size with coal of the calorific value available (averaging about 11000 BTU/lb) taxed the physical endurance of a fireman and it is arguable that mechanical stoking might have increased their effectiveness, though not their efficiency. Nevertheless it must be emphasised again that it was only relatively to the 110's that they were disappointing and although only eleven of the 210's were built there were a hundred and ten 310's. Many worked, however, on what were to become Czechoslovak routes and only forty-three passed to BBO but twenty-four were still in service in 1951.

As a footnote to these observations it is perhaps of interest to note that in 1904 on the KFNB Rayl and Simon produced a design for a four cylinder compound Pacific with a view to taking the heavy day dining car expresses (200–230 tonnes) from Vienna to Cracow in seven hours. Essentially they would have been an enlarged version of Gölsdorf's 108 class 4-4-2's, using 1840mm driving wheels but the design would have yielded a grate area 25% less than in the Class 210 2-6-4's and 0.50 square metres less than the Class 110's by which they would undoubtedly have been outclassed. The design was never carried out, however, but had it been built it would have been as elegant in appearance as the Bavarian Pacifics.

Consideration of express passenger locomotives has led our account far ahead of where the account of tank and freight locomotive design was left. The last tank class to be mentioned was the Class 30 originally designed with the Vienna Stadtbahn in mind. The class which followed it was designed as a successor to the sundry classes of aged locomotives inherited by the kk St. B ekeing out the fag-ends of their lives on lightly laid and sharply curved branches and industrial sidings. This was the 99 Class of 2-6-0 tanks designed in 1897 and built at intervals, in saturated steam and superheated versions, until 1914 by which times the state railways had eighty-nine of them and the Niederosterreichische Landesbahnen a further fourteen scattered all over the system. Dimensionally they were very small: two cylinders 370 and 570mm diameter ×570mm stroke, driving wheels 1120mm diameter, grate area 1.42 square metres and heating surface 82 square metres. The coupled wheelbase was only 2.80m, little more than the distance between the leading and the first coupled axle (2.25m). The original examples had the twin domes and link pipe which were their designer's trademark but later examples and replacement boilers had a single dome.

For the next five years the tank engine seems to have been passed over in the production programme in favour of the developments, already related, in heavy goods and express passenger locomotives but in 1904 the first of the 129's appeared, a 2-6-0 intermediate tank engine with 1614mm driving wheels, capable of a quite surprising speed yet good on acceleration away from stops. The cylinder arrangement selected was the two cylinder compound (420 and 650×720mm), the pressure 14 Atmospheres but a much smaller grate (2.0 square metres) and heating surface (106.1 square metres) than those used in the express tender locomotives. The 2-6-0 wheel arrangement, however, allowed only a very limited coal capacity and two years later the class was redesigned with a trailing axle and a much larger bunker, extending the range of the engines and allowing them to undertake intermediate express work. In this form they were known as the 229 Class and the locomotives of the original design were rebuilt to conform being then designated 229.40 Class. The superheated version, first built in 1912, was given the classification 29. There were thirty six of the 29's and one hundred and sixty two of the 229's plus further examples on the Sudbahn (11) and the Vienna – Aspang Bahn (10). Of the total, ninety eventually came into BBO ownership, though the ten from the Aspang Bahn did not do so until the owning railway was taken over in 1937, and the last seven were in service until 1961.

Mention of the Aspang Bahn (known as the EWA – Eisenbahn Wien Aspang) is a reminder of a class which insinuated itself into the kk St. B from small beginnings on the Schneebergbahn, opened in 1898 from Wiener Neustadt to Puchberg but worked from 1st January, 1899 by the EWA. Krauss of Linz supplied it, in 1898, with a 0-8-0 two cylinder compound tank locomotive in which the influence, if not the actual hand, of Gölsdorf was very apparent. Pressed to 13 Atmospheres it had 420 and 650×570mm cylinder, 1,140mm driving wheels and 1.65 square metres of grate area coupled to a total heating surface of 99.75 square metres. Although the wheelbase was only 3,70m it had side play arranged on Helmholtz's principle. Being flexible and light on its feet (with an axle loading of less than 12,000kg) the design was taken up by the kk St. B where the class reached a total of one hundred and sixty two locomotives, designated 178. When the locomotive stock was split up in 1921 sixty six of them came to the BBO, the last of which was not withdrawn until 1969.

The operating department appears to have formed the idea *c.* 1905/6, or to have adopted it from Germany, of using a class of light, fast tank locomotives to haul trains of two or three or even four light coaches at express speeds over short distances. Possibly they had in mind parts of the old KEB mainline where a number of stations were awkwardly placed on gradients or curves making it necessary to provide trains with more locomotive power than they would otherwise have required simply to enable them to start. Whatever the reason Gölsdorf was asked to provide two locomotives to enable the experiments to be conducted. What he provided was Class 112 a 2-2-2 well tank design, not unlike a Norris translated into the twentieth century, a two cylinder compound with 260 and 400×550mm cylinders and 1450mm driving wheels. For the first time he made use of a smoke box reheater coil to boost the temperature of the steam on its way between the cylinders providing 3.29 square metres of additional heating (or, perhaps warming?) surface in addition to the 52.16 square metres of normal heating surface. For such a small engine, the total weight of which was only 31,600kg, it had a remarkably large firebox (1.03 square metres of grate) by comparison, say, with a Class 99, 0-6-2, which, as noted earlier had only 1.42 square metres and was 2 Atmospheres less in working pressure into the bargain.

The experiments seem not to have convinced the operating side that anything was to be gained by multiplying the class and consequently the initial two remained alone. They ended their days under the Deutsche Reichsbahn stationed at Hütteldorf (West Vienna) and used, inter alia, on push and pull trains from the Westbahnhof to Unter Purkersdorf.

By contrast it is interesting to take a brief look at the class of sixteen simple expansion two cylinder 2-8-0 tanks which St. EG built for their own use in 1908 in banking and marshalling duties. Valuing, as on earlier occasions in such a situation, ease of handling and reversing before maximum thermal efficiency they used a pressure of only 11 Atmospheres, 450×600m cylinders and 1120mm driving wheels. Never having had the satisfaction of seeing one, so to speak, in the flesh your author feels that it was a design that would have looked quite at home in Feltham Marshalling Yard alongside the five 4-6-2 tanks. What happened in the event was that almost as they came out the railway was nationalised (in October 1909) with the result that no more were built, and at the division of locomotives post 1918 those that had been put into service became the property of CSD.

The KFNB had already been taken into the kk St. B in October 1906 so that the Sudbahn was the only major railway outside the state fold and it thus fell to Karl Gölsdorf to initiate all new designs for the expanding traffic of the state system. In 1908 Louis Gölsdorf gave up the post of chief mechanical engineer of the Sudbahn and was succeeded by E. Prossy who had a much more critical approach to compounding and inside cylinders. Whereas, therefore, locomotive practice on the Sudbahn and kk St. B had been, for some years, all but identical from 1908 onward it began to diverge again.

Economically the country thrust ahead with consequent increase in all classes of rail traffic. In palace and parliamentary affairs it was, however, set on a path to catastrophe with all the inevitability of Greek tragedy. The aging Emperor kept court at the Schönbrunn whilst his heir apparent, the Crown Prince Ferdinand, kept virtually a rival establishment at the Belvedere in almost flagrant opposition letting it be at·least an open secret that on his succession to the throne he would institute drastically revised policies in Imperial Affairs. In politics the country and Parliament was riven between German speakers and non-Germans, between Catholics and Protestants and between Left and Right. In the midst of this, in the seven or eight years of peace left, Gölsdorf managed to create some of the most brilliant designs of locomotive the world had seen to that time.

Of these the first to be noticed is the 280 Class 2-10-0's of 1906 built by St. EG. In designing them Gölsdorf initially had in mind the taxing eastern approach to the Arlberg with its long climbs of 2.6% ruling gradient over which he wished them to work 300 tonne trains at speeds of 30 to 34km/hour, whilst at the same time having the ability to maintain 70km/hour in safety over less arduous stretches. In them he used the same cylinders and arrangement as in the Class 110 2-6-2's but with a bigger boiler, the largest then in use on the Continent, pressed to 16 Atmospheres and containing a grate area of 4.60 square metres and a total heating surface of 250 square metres. Though the driving wheels, at 1450mm, might have been thought small by passenger train standards they did not prevent the locomotives living up to their designer's expectations of speed capability. The 280's were fitted with Clench type smokebox steam dryers but the subsequent 380's, the fully superheated version first built in 1909, had Schmidt firetube superheaters boosting the evaporative area by some 20%.

So well did the 280's and 380's perform that they were soon to be found on the newly opened Tauern route, the Karawanken and the Pyrrnbahn from Linz to Selzthal. Although totalling only twenty six locomotives (both 280's and 380's) they had a fame that bordered on the world-wide. Fourteen of them were attached to Triest for working over the Wocheinerbahn and stayed there at the post 1918 division of rolling stock. The remaining twelve came into BBO stock and lasted just into DR days.

They had two sequels. On the kk St. B they led on, by the operation of logic, to the even larger Class 100 2-12-0 of 1911 in which four cylinders 450 and 760×680mm were used and the pressure was 16 Atmospheres. The grate in this boiler was just over three metres in length and its area 5.0 square metres, a formidable task indeed for a fireman. Like the 380's the boiler had a Schmidt superheater of an area of 47 square metres and the general heating surface was 249 square metres. The length over buffers was 13,190mm. Allocated to the Triest division the first and only example was stationed at Görz. The intention, had the war not intervened, was to use the class also over the Tauernbahn but because of the post-war electrification scheme this never came to pass. As a less direct sequel it is likely that the German Class 58's of 1917 must have drawn on the experience created by the solitary Class 100 though in detail it remained unique.

The 380's also had a sequel. Prossy on the Sudbahn is said to have distrusted their complication so that whereas a few years before under Louis Gölsdorf, examples of the design would soon have been at work on that railway the situation in 1911 was somewhat different. Whilst respecting their behaviour as steam generators and as vehicles Prossy desired something less sophisticated in the engine department and for this he turned to H. Steffan, chief designer (and later a technical director) at St. EG, who produced for him the 580's, two cylinder superheated simples using 610×720 cylinders and a pressure of 14 Atmospheres, in a boiler marginally larger in combined heating surface. One of the features of the design was the size of the piston valves, the diameter of which was 320mm.

Since no formal comparative performance tests were made there is no way of knowing how well Prossy's 580's compared with the 380's. Personal rivalry seems not to have been present in any form between the two CME's and no claims were made for either design at the other's expense. Aside from his preference for simple over compound expansion Prossy seems sincerely to have approved of and admired the work of his senior confrere and never was there a desire by either to score points off the other. History provided an answer to at least one aspect of the speculation. Thirty years later the 580's were in full vigour hauling heavy trains to the south rampart of the Semmering whilst the three survivors of the 380's were relegated to secondary freight duties. Even this circumstance is difficult to evaluate objectively as in the post war period, successively under Johann Rihosek and Lehner the BBO policy turned away from compounding and particularly from four cylinder compounds which must have loaded the dice against the 380's but it is also said that the inside drive of the 380's and the need to pare every available kilogram off the frame weight had acted together to reduce the rigidity in their frames to a level where they were appreciably heavier on maintenance than the 580's.

Of the twenty seven 580's which came into BBO hands twenty four were still working in 1951 and the last went on for a further ten years. A batch of them went to Greece in the mid fifties to help out whilst the Greeks' newly built Italian 2-10-2's – probably the greatest white elephant of post war locomotive building – were rebuilt. Greece had already had a batch of 580's new in the mid-twenties.

In noticing the progression of development of the express and intermediate classes we have failed to give notice to a number of very interesting classes designed solely for freight. We have already discussed the origin of the 2-10-0's of 180 Class in 1900, the first Austrian ten coupler, constructed on Helmholtz's theory of side play in the coupled axles compensated by lateral articulation in the coupling rods.

Their extraordinarily large cylinders, 560 and 850×632mm, were the largest used on any Gölsdorf design and certainly admissible in such sizes only because of the low speeds for which the locomotives were intended. At the time Gölsdorf was using 14 Atmospheres pressure and stuck to this for the 180's right through to the final fully superheated version (the 80's) in 1911. The grate area throughout was 3.42 square metres. In the original version the heating surface was 203.30 square metres but in the superheated boiler the combined hearing surface was 177 square metres of which 26.8 square metres was in the superheater. Though the early boilers had the double dome and connector pipe, replacement boilers and those used on the later built examples dispensed with it. The initial batch were put to hauling heavy mineral trains in Bohemia and Moravia but so well did they perform that within ten years they were to be found in most other parts of the system. The Triest and Villach divisions had considerable allocations, Innsbruck, Vienna and Linz a number, the latter mostly shedded at Budweis (now Czech). The Lemberg division also had a substantial allocation. After the breaking up of the kk St. B in 1918 the 80's and 180's were probably the most widely distributed class. The last survivors in Austria lasted until 1967 but in Czechoslovakia examples went on longer still. Their fate was settled as much by the administrative decisions to move out of steam as by their age or design.

During these years the Class 60 2-6-0 tender locomotives continued to be built and in 1905 the class was updated as the 60.500, the most noticeable difference being the discarding of the "lifting handle" arrangement of twin domes and a connecting pipe in favour of a single dome on the rear ring and a steam take off where the second dome would once have been found. The appearance of these latest additions to the ranks of Class 60 coincided almost exactly with the appearance from First Bohemian of an even more compact design of 2-6-0 for the Bohemian Northern notable for being the first Austrian tender locomotive to be equipped with a Schmidt superheater, first used in Austrian territory on a class of 0-6-0T locomotive which Krauss delivered to the Bukowinaer Lokalbahnen in 1904. Space and our terms of reference bar further discussion here of either type.

Superheating had been gaining ground in German speaking Europe for some years. Schmidt had built smokebox superheaters in the mid nineties and Gölsdorf had been experimentally using the smokebox superheater on the kk St. B in 1904. Hammel, the progressive director of Maffei in Munich, was also an advocate of superheating. The Class 329 2-6-2's built first at Floridsdorf in 1907 for goods and express goods work in the more easily graded areas of Bohemia and Moravia and in the territories of the former Nordbahn and Nord West Bahn had smokebox superheaters but since virtually the whole class worked outside the limits of modern Austria and none accrued to the Republic we need not give them extended notice.

To return to the Mogul type, however, it should be mentioned that the St. EG which had been building 2-6-0's since 1899 built a three cylinder compound version (Class 38.5) in 1903 using a single inside high pressure and two low pressures (490 and 580×650mm) and a working pressure of 13 Atmospheres followed by the next year with the 38's a design of very comparable proportions, on the same frames and running gear but two cylinder simples (520×650mm) still at 13 Atmospheres pressure but using a Schmidt smoketube superheater with 33.5 square metres of superheating surface, finding them so much superior in their performance that forty three of them were built compared with only ten of the 38.5 class. Two of the 38.5 class (later kk St. B 660) went to BBO and they lasted only until 1925 whilst all the 38 Class (kk St. B Class 760) went to CSD.

It is also appropriate to notice the simple expansion two cylinder 2-6-0's of the ONWB (later kk St. B Class 460) delivered by Floridsdorf in 1906. These had full Schmidt smoketube superheaters (29.9 square metres) but still only 13 Atmospheres boiler pressure. With 510×632mm cylinders they were a shade smaller than the St. EG Class 38's but rather crisper performers. Twenty three were built and being on the territory of the new republic when the Armistice was signed they stayed there but, unlike many minority classes, they were a popular and acceptable addition to the rolling stock. Six were lost to Austria during the 1939/45 war but the last survivor was not withdrawn until 1961.

Not long after the ONWB 2-6-0's Gölsdorf produced a further variation on a well worked theme by producing three further 60 Class locomotives in a sub-class (given the classification 60.80) fitted with the Pielock superheater in the body of the boiler barrel. In giving them a superheater area of just under 18 square metres the designer sacrificed some 21 square metres of conventional tube heating surface and if we may draw any conclusion from the fact that only three were built it must be that Gölsdorf found them inferior in performance to locomotives equipped with Schmidt smoketube superheaters.

Gölsdorf's final design for mountain express work – in fact his last design with high power output – was the 470 class launched in 1914, a 2-8-2 with 1614mm drivers intended to relieve the Classes 9 and 10 of the heaviest duties. Four cylinder compounds, they had the same arrangement of valve gear and piston valves as the Class 310 2-6-4's the piston valves on each side (which were 450mm in diameter) serving two cylinders. The cylinders were 450×690mm in diameter ×680mm stroke and the pressure used was 15 Atmospheres. Following his recent practice Gölsdorf arranged the drive onto the third axle which meant a very long connecting rod each side. As they were intended for moderate speeds he used Adams leading and trailing axles in lieu of the more flexible but heavier Helmholtz pony truck as on the 310's. The grate area was 4.5 square metres, the plain heating surface 191.1 square metres, and the Schmidt-superheater surfaces were 49.4 square metres.

The 470's were not a happy class and external circumstances were against them. They appeared just as war broke out in 1914 so that no test results are available but it seems probable that they suffered from the same trouble as the 310's, namely they were beyond the capacity of a fireman to fire to maximum power output at lower speeds. How Gölsdorf reacted to them is not known, nor what he might have done with the class had he lived. The one remaining passenger tender engine design which he produced before his death – the Class 910 – he provided with two simple expansion cylinders so perhaps this is an indication of his disappointment in the 470's but the 910's were built for service outside the present confines of Austria and are outside our present terms of reference. What happened to the twelve 470's that survived to serve the Republic is narrated in the next Chapter.

The beneficial effect of medium superheat – 350° to 365° seems to have been about the maximum attained – as applied to the immediately pre-war designs seems to have impressed itself very deeply upon both Gölsdorf and Prossy, agreed as they were upon also every aspect of design other than the use of compounding. It seems likely that had the former lived he might have channelled his thought on future designs in the direction of the superheated two cylinder simple favoured by Prossy and adopted after his death by his successor, and associate for many years before that, Johann Rihosek.

In 1913 Prossy had produced the first of an outstandingly successful 4-6-2T design using rather lower boiler pressure (13 Atmospheres) and two 475×720mm simple expansion cylinders. Perhaps the most surprising feature, in the dimensional sense, was the relatively small grate (2.7 square metres) about the same as the 60.800 series 2-6-0 tender locomotives of the kk St. B the boilers of which were nearly 10% less in heating surface. In the 629's the general heating surfaces was 140.8 square metres plus a further 29.1 square metres in the superheater. Helped by the absence of a cranked axle and inside motion work Prossy managed to keep the gross weight down to 80,200kg. Distributed over the six axles this gave an average axle loading of only 13,400kg but in fact the loading of the three driving axles was rather higher averaging 14,400kg each, even so keeping well within the Sudbahn and kk St. B limit.

With alterations to the boiler the design was adopted by Gölsdorf for the kk St. B almost as he died. The changes in the boiler enforced by the wartime shortage of copper were brought about by the substitution of a steel box. On the state railway systems of the newly independent Poland and Czechoslovakia they were found to be very acceptable for both ordinary passenger and intermediate express working and both countries went on producing them. In the case of the Czechs the last was made in 1941 giving the class a total production run of 28 years. On their home territory they were multiplied under Rihosek in the inter-war years until BBO, having kept forty after the Armistice and acquired another fifteen with the Sudbahn, had a total of eighty five. Ten were still in service when steam traction ceased.

By the time they came out on the kk St. B in 1917 Austria was in extremely low water militarily and civil disaffection was running high. These events and their consequences which were external to the railways dictated the course of locomotive policy to a large degree. Had these devastating events not occurred, however, there still remains the question of what would have happened if Gölsdorf had not died in 1916 at the very young age of 55. One has to do a double "suppose" exercise. Suppose there had been no war and consequent dismantling of the kingdom and empire and suppose that Gölsdorf had remained alive and in office how, one asks, would locomotive policy have evolved. In one respect at least it is tempting to deduce that it would have turned out in pretty much the way that it did despite his death. There is at least a suggestion in the final designs – his own 910's and his adoption of Prossy's 629's – that the attraction of simple expansion plus superheat would have eclipsed his earlier and sustained interest in compounding. Clearly Johann Rihosek had come to this conclusion, for this is the course he implemented as soon as he had the chance, though he scarcely had time to accustom himself to office as Gölsdorf had known it since after only just over two years he was reduced from command of a locomotive stud of over seven thousand on the old kk St. B to that of one of less than 2400 on the new BBO. Whether or not Gölsdorf would have been able to adapt himself to such hampering conditions is perhaps questionable. The fact that the BBO inherited rather more than 150 classes of locomotive from the kk St. B was largely a reflection of the fact that the latter was an agglomeration of many companies rather than a consequence of Gölsdorf's policy.

By 1918 the conditions under which he had worked had undergone a reverse. Rail transport had ceased to expand and the pressure to produce faster and more powerful locomotives had lessened. Moreover road transport, as a competitor, had undergone rapid development during the war. The observer looking back to his tenure of office, from the vantage point of nearly seventy five years of hindsight, cannot come to a conclusion other than that he would have felt circumscribed and hemmed-in by the circumstances and confines of the Republic. This is, however, merely conjecture. As it is he is remembered as a genial man, talented to the point of brilliance, and broad-minded to boot whose death brought sorrow even to those whom the war had made his country's enemies.

After his death in 1916 and the accession of Johann Rihosek (1869–1956) to his chair the reverses to which the empire and kingdom were already being subjected were added to. The Emperor died on 21st November, 1916 and was succeeded by his grand nephew Karl Franz but the military situation the latter inherited had become beyond redemption. Left to herself Austria might well have sued for peace in 1917 but the Germans understandably perhaps, would not permit the idea to be entertained and peace did not come until the Armistice of 11th November, 1918. The following day the Republic was proclaimed. It is an easy thing to set down, sixty three years later, such an event as if it were possible to do such a thing at a stroke, to call into being at a moments notice all the minutae of practical administration that make orderly government possible. At least in Hungary and Austria there was the apparatus of central government and its institutions whereas in the new countries, Poland, Czechoslavia and Yugoslavia these had to be constructed.

So far as the railways were concerned the administrations clutched to themselves what they found to hand and endeavoured to hold onto it. Austria simply took and used the locomotives that were physically on her new territory and from this basic stock evolved a new policy to meet the changed times. How this was constructed is the subject matter of Chapter V and it is convenient here to break off for a survey in the next chapter of rack and other special locomotives, steam railcars and the locomotives of the lokalbahnen, both standard and narrow gauge.

Chapter V
Rack, special and narrow gauge locomotives

The Kahlenberg is an eminence of the Vienna Woods to the north west of Vienna giving views over the wine villages of Grinzing and Nussdorf, the Danube and the more distant city itself. In 1529, in the church on the summit, Charles V and his nobles dedicated themselves before descending to the plain to defeat the Turks then laying siege to Vienna. It was and is popular with the Viennese as a resort and as a place of residence for the well off and to its summit ascended the first rack railway in Austria, the standard gauge Kahlenbergbahn begun in the year of the Austrian financial crisis, 1873, and opened in 1874 worked by six locomotives supplied by the Swiss Locomotive Works, Winterthur, using boilers built in Leeds by John Fowler. Unlike most of the more recent rack lines in Austria it was constructed on the Riggenback system – the central iron ladder up which the locomotives climbed, figuratively, hand over hand – and the wheels which bore on the running rails were for carrying only. The ruling gradient, 10%, was not too far outside the capabilities of adhesion working and in consequence the locomotives normally headed their trains. Service braking was done by a band brake and by means of the engine cylinders which were equipped with water sprays for cooling but the trailing axle was hand-braked and the coaches had a hand-brake worked by the guard who rode on a garden-type seat on the roof.

Constructionally the locomotives were distinctive in having a very high firebox surmounted, unusually for Austria, by Ramsbottom safety valves, spring balances being the general rule then and for another thirty years until Gölsdorf introduced the Coales pop safety valve. The boiler had a grate area of 1.1 square metres and heating surface of 53.80 square metres and was pressed to 9 Atmospheres;, the cylinders were 300mm×450mm. The line ran more or less unaltered for nearly fifty years and closed in 1922 in the period of depression following the end of the War. Though the line was standard gauge and had goods wagons and the station at Nussdorf was but a short distance from Nussdorf station on the Franz Josef Bahn there was no link line and the Kahlenbergbahn lived out its life in isolation.

The Riggenbach system was also used on the rather later metre gauge Gaisbergbahn opened in 1887 at Salzburg for which the locomotives were supplied by Esslingen. No. 1 (Works No. 2205) is preserved under cover at the Vienna Technical Museum. The basic arrangement of the working parts is very much as in the Kahlenberg locomotives but the use of outside frames and side tanks gives the Gaisbergbahn design an altogether sturdier appearance. The line on which they ran came to an end in 1928.

A little to the west of the Gaisbergbahn the combined rack and adhesion Achenseebahn, also metre gauge, climbs on the rack from the junction with the main line at Jenbach to the summit at Eben (970m) and then continues by adhesion to the landing stage on the Achensee. Opened in 1889 this used the Riggenbach system but subsequent rack lines in Austria used the Abt rack system. The locomotives were supplied by Floridsdorf, the first in 1889.

The dimensions of the Gaisbergbahn locomotives were a little larger than on the Kahlenbergbahn – the boilers had $57.9m^2$ of heating surface, $1.28m^2$ of grate area and were pressed to 11 atmospheres whilst the cylinders were the same in bore (350mm) but 50mm greater in the stroke (500mm) – but those at Achensee were substantially smaller, $50m^2$ heating surface, $92m^2$ of grate and cylinders 330×500mm though the working pressure of 11 atmospheres was maintained.

The two other mountain rack railways in Austria, the Schafbergbahn and the Hochschneebergbahn were also metre gauge, the former opened in 1893 and the latter in 1896. The Schafbergbahn was originally part of the undertaking of the mainly 760mm Salzkammergut Lokalbahn and was taken over by DRB in 1939. The locomotives used on each were supplied by Krauss from the Linz works. Built as 0-4-2T's they have the cylinders placed at midpoint between (and above) the coupled axles, with the piston rod facing forward and driving a vertical oscillating link from which the pinions are powered, thus making it possible to increase the stroke to 600mm, the bore being decreased to 320mm. Although the boilers are smaller, giving only 36m² of heating surface compared with 50m² at Achensee, the grate area remains the same, but the power output is increased by the boiler pressure of 14 Atmospheres. The lever action of the oscillating links increases the 11 tonne piston thrust by about two thirds.

The Schafbergbahn was almost totally a tourist line but the Schneebergbahn was an all the year round line with intermediate stopping places serving the local population.

Both look insignificant, however, by comparison with the rack and adhesion working of the Erzbergbahn, the line from Vordernberg to Eisenerz linking the iron ore quarrying operation at Eisenertz with the steelworks complex at Donawicz – Leoben, 20km long with a maximum gradient of 7% (1 in 14). For working this line the kk St. B administration produced a class of 0-6-2 combined rack and adhesion tank locomotives, in production from 1890 to 1908 by which time eighteen had been built, given the class number 69. Dimensionally they were very much larger than any other rack locomotives in Austria but used only 11 atmospheres pressure. The total boiler heating surface was 131,64m² served by 2.10m² of grate. The rack engine had 480mm×500mm cylinders and a rack pinion diameter of 688mm. The adhesion engine had 420mm×450mm cylinders and used 1050mm driving wheels. Examples of this class and the following 269 class, described below, were the last standard gauge steam locomotives to run in regular revenue earning service on ÖBB.

With the progressive development of the mine and the steelworks in the first decade of this century the traffic necessitated double heading by two of the 0-6-2's as well as a pusher at the rear. Because of this increase in traffic Gölsdorf designed the 269 Class 0-12-0T with 1050mm diameter driving wheels again with combined rack and adhesion, of which three examples were built by Floridsdorf in 1912. In them the rack engine, driving two rack pinions, was placed between the third and fourth driving axles, powered by two cylinders 420×450mm situated in an inclined position under the smokebox. The adhesion cylinders (570×520mm) were placed horizontally outside, driving, by a characteristically Gölsdorf long connecting rod, the fourth coupled axle. For both rack and adhesion engines Heusinger (Walschaert's) valve gear was used but the inside gear worked through rocking shafts. These formidable locomotives worked at 13 Atmospheres but though they had 195.65 square metres of heating surface, served by 3.3 square metres of grate, they had no superheater. The overall length was 12.45m. Having been the world's most powerful rack locomotives for three decades they were eventually eclipsed by the two locomotives of ÖBB Class 297 built, as will be noted in the next chapter, by the DRB administration in 1941.

The question may be asked why Gölsdorf forsook compounding in designing these locomotives. A little reflection, however, shows that it must almost certainly have been considerations of space. To obtain from a compound the power output he was seeking would have necessitated the use of his four cylinder arrangement but the space inside the frames was already pre-empted by the rack engine. Why did he not use superheating, upon the merits of which he had, at that time, come to a firm favourable decision? Probably he wished, again from the point of view of practical arrangement, to use slide valves in preference to the piston valves which would have been inevitable had he employed superheated steam.

To turn our backs, for a brief space, on main line practice, it is an interesting contrast to consider the motive power of the lokalbahnen, both standard and narrow gauge. The Muhlkreisbahn, running north from its own station in North Linz to near the Czech border at Aigen Schlagel, can never have been anything but a defiant act of local patriotism by its creator, Baron Lazarini, nor can it ever, even in the infancy of its traffic, have been an easy line for its locomotives, with its 4.6% ruling grade and, once it forsook the Danube, its succession of steep climbs and descents. To work it Krauss supplied from their Linz works five light 0-6-0T locomotives with short side tanks and further tanks between the frames. Because continuous brakes were not a legal necessity on a lokalbahn they began life with counter-pressure brakes but after the working of the line was taken over by the state in 1900 vacuum apparatus was fitted. They had 335×400 cylinders and a boiler carrying 12 Atmospheres pressure, with 75 square metres of heating surface and a grate area of 1.08 square metres. Doubtless the fact that the driving wheels were only 915mm diameter helped them to cope with the ups and downs of their native line on which they remained the motive power for some forty years, latterly as Class 494 of the BBO, kept in sole charge by the fact that the bridges would take nothing heavier until the BBO carried out some strengthening in the twenties. They were withdrawn c. 1930 and No. 2 (Krauss Works No. 1901, kk St. B. 494.62) is preserved (see Chapter VII).

Small though they were they were not the smallest branch line locomotives. The Niederösterriechische Landesbahnen, which had eighteen 2-6-0T of kk St. B Classes 99, 199 and 399, had also nine 0-4-0T, the earliest dating from 1897 and taken over from Munz, the railway contractor, at the opening from Ganserndorf to Gaweinstal in 1903. They were all used on this and the other slightly graded and lightly trafficked routes Korneuburg to Ernstbrunn and Siebenbrunn to Orth. Though they were superseded on train duties when the Federal Railways took over the working of the Landesbahnen in 1922 they had a relatively long life as shed pilots and the last ran until 1967.

The Niederösterreichische Sudwestbahnen also used 0-4-0T locomotives. Apart from one Krauss (Munich) tram engine these consisted of six side tanks by Wiener Neustadt dating from 1880/81. All of basically similar dimensions (240×400mm outside cylinders, 30 square metres of heating surface, 0.65 square grate area, 12 Atmospheres pressure and 850mm wheels) they differed a little in the design of cab used in the second batch and by its having the dome transposed from the rear ring to the front ring of the boiler. They were absorbed into kk St. B stock in 1882 when the state took over the line, as soon almost as they were delivered. Mostly they had been sold by 1907, though one survived to become the property of CSD in 1918. Another, sold in 1907, was bought for use by the military railway regiment at Korneuberg. The real work horses of the NOSWB were two classes of 0-6-0 tender locomotive (later kk St. B Classes 91 and 92) totalling sixteen in all, twelve of which were built by Wiener Neustadt in 1876 and 1877, the last four (of Class 92) in 1888 by which time they were distinctly archaic. The 91's were slightly smaller in the boiler (89.21 square metres against 102 square metres in heating surface and 1.37 square metres against 1.41 square metres in the grate area) and had 1200mm wheels compared with 1300mm in the 92's which were used for many of the passenger trains. The last to survive (until 1937) was a 92 of the original 1876 batch whilst one of the first scrapped, in 1927, was a 92 class from 1888.

Narrow gauge local railways – apart from the Linz to Gmunden line already discussed in Chapert II – were mainly products of the 1887 lokalbahn legislation and were with trifling exceptions, all opened in the period covered by this chapter. The Steyrtalbahn (opened in stages beginning in 1889) led the ranks both chronologically and also in the locomotive department, where, by using Krauss – built 0-6-2 side tanks with great success it laid a foundation of practice which subsequent lines were to follow. The Salzkammergut Lokalbahn indeed used an almost identical design but with a slightly larger boiler for their numbers 3–5 and the same again apart from a shorter smokebox and further increase in boiler capacity for their Nos. 6–11 inclusive. As designed in 1888 the class had the coal bunkers between the side tanks and the cab front, the dome on the front ring with the sand box behind, the extended smokebox, already mentioned, which gave the engines a distinctly pregnant appearance, a Krauss type pony truck and cable worked friction brakes involving guide pullies on the chimney, smokebox front and cab top. Later examples, such as Steyrtalbahn No. 6, had the bunker transferred to the conventional position behind the cab, a somewhat shorter smokebox and the side tanks carried forward to the line of the smokebox door. The cylinders of these locomotives were 290×400mm, the heating surface 40.15 square metres and grate area 0.80 square metres.

The earliest kk St. B 0-6-2T type, also from Krauss, for the 760mm gauge, the T class used on the Gurktalbahn from 1898 and the Kühnsdorf – Eisenkappel from 1902, was somewhat smaller in every respect using 640mm driving wheels (where the Steyrtalbahn had used 800mm) and 260×300mm cylinders compared with 290×400mm. The heating surface and grate area at 26.9 square metres and 0.60 square metres respectively were also markedly less. The three examples on the Gurktalbahn ran until 1959/60. The T class was, however, soon abandoned for the U's built in essentially similar form from 1897 through to 1913 by which time the class total for greater Austria was forty-three of which twenty-one remained in the republic after 1918. They were used on the Ybbstalbahn, the Murtalbahn, the Bregenzerwaldbahn, the NÖLB and the Weiz-Birkfeld. They were also shuffled about after the German occupation of Czechoslovakia, Austria and Jugoslavia, in 1938–41. Thus U29 and U30 originally on the Spalato-Sinj line and taken by Jugoslavia after 1918 were brought back into Austria itself in 1942 for use on the Steiermarkische Landesbahnen. Most of the U's were built as might have been expected, by Krauss at Linz but five (U25–U29) were built by St. EG and two (U33 and U34) which never served in metropolitan Austria, by First Bohemian. Though the driving wheel and cylinder dimensions of the U's were the same as on the Steyrtalbahn 0-6-2's the boiler was rather larger; containing 46.3 square metres of heating surface and 1 square metre of grate area compared, in the latter, with 40.15 square metres and 0.80 square metres respectively.

Given the Austrian interest in compounding it was, perhaps, inevitable that a compound version of the U's should be produced though there is no evidence that Gölsdorf had any direct hand in it. The first examples were ordered in 1902 by the NOLB for service in the north west corner of the province between Gmund and Gross Gerungs where a rather more powerful locomotive was needed and they were also used by the same owners on the Mank to Ruprechtshofen line whilst the independent Zillertalbahn's No. 3 (1902) was of the same design. Though reflecting the trend of Austrian Government railway thought the actual design of the compound U's, referred to as the Uv's, was the work of the Krauss drawing office. In them the boiler was enlarged to give 57.8 square metres of heating surface compared with 46.3 square metres in the U's and 320 and 500 by 400 cylinders were used.

Driving wheels and the general profile of the locomotives, except for modified cab roofs, remained as in the later U's. Locomotive Uv7 (ÖBB 298.207) was, at the time of writing, still in service at Gmund having passed successfully its thorough boiler inspection in 1980.

Four couplers, on the whole, made little headway on Austrian lines of 760mm gauge. There were two by Krauss, Linz on the SKLB, built in 1890 and used for the short branch from Ischl to Strobl, one of which lived until 1953, though the other became a casualty of war service in 1914/18. The Steiermarkische Landesbahnen had four, also by Krauss, in 1892, two for the Preding-Stainz and two for the Poltschack-Gonobitz-Hohlenstein (ceded to Yugoslavia). These were generally similar in wheels and cylinders (760mm wheels and 225×350mm cylinders) but the boilers were a little different, those of the St. LB having larger fireboxes (0.51 square metres of grate area against 0.43 square metres on the SKGLB) at the expense of shorter tubes and hence a reduction in general heating surface from 23.4 square metres to 21.6 square metres. The second of the Preding-Stainz examples (Krauss No. 2774) was rebuilt in 1969 for one man operation and is now on the Murtalbahn. Nor were 0-6-0T more numerous, the only examples to have a long life being three for the St. LB Kapfenberg-Au line. One of these three (Krauss No. 2885) was sold in 1973 to the 760 Club for preservation and is now kept on the Murtalbahn. The NÖLB also had a couple of very small 0-6-0T of industrial type, one by Krauss, Linz (1909) and the other by Wiener Neustadt (1907), the former with 580mm wheels, the latter 610mm. They also differed in cylinder bore (210 and 225 respectively) though the stroke (300mm) was the same in each. Weighing 11 and 11.7 tonnes respectively they were about the same as the StmLB 0-4-0's.

Eight couplers were scarcely more numerous comprising only the interesting 0-8-4 type semi-articulated locomotives built for the Mariazellerbahn, six of which are still used on the Waldviertalbahn. The reason for adopting the type is not entirely clear since they are effactually 0-8-0 tender engines with a four wheeled tender close coupled by sliding arm attachments on either side of the firebox which cause them to cling to the locomotive rather like a cautious (or affectionate!) pillion rider to a motor cyclist. Since they are used without turning they presumably rank as tank engines and over-come some official encumbrance to the running of tender engines in reverse. They are rated for a maximum speed of 40kph. The surviving six are all of class Mh with 410×450mm simple expansion cylinders and 900mm driving wheels. Their boilers have 78.85 square metres of heating surface and 1.50 square metres of grate area. The original four came from Krauss, Linz in 1906, followed in 1907 by two of class Mv, the compound version with 370 and 500mm diameter cylinders and 95.04 square metres of heating surface, and by two more simples in 1908. One of the compounds was scrapped in 1964, the second in 1973. The further development of eight couplers and the arrival of ten couplers on the 760mm gauge in Austria were, however, events of the twenties and of the succeeding Chapter.

Metre gauge in Austria – apart from the various rack lines – was mainly electric save for the steeply graded Mittelgebirgsbahn from Innsbruck to Igls. Here again, because of the steep gradients (4.6%) and very sharp curvature, the Klose system was adopted in three 0-6-2 by Krauss, Linz, two from 1900 and the third from 1901. All ran until the line was electrified in 1936. In cylinders and wheels these locomotives were very similar to a 760mm gauge Uv (viz 800mm driving wheels, 320 and 500×400mm cylinders), but the boilers with 46.3 square metres of heating surface and 1 square metre of grate were the same as a U.

Finally, before leaving narrow gauge steam locomotives, mention ought to be made of the four compound 2-4-0T built by Krauss, Linz, for the Lambach-Gmunden (1106mm gauge) in

1895–99. When the line was regauged to standard in 1903 these locomotives were regauged with it to become Class 189 of the kk St. B and one of them lasted long enough to receive a DRB number.

Steam railcars on the standard gauge in pre 1918 greater Austria worked, almost without exception, in what is now Czechoslovakia. Though few lived beyond the 1920's 1.401 built in 1908 and attached to the Prerau division of the kk St. B in the days of old Austria, ran until 1948 as CSD 223.001. The builder of most of the limited number of steam railcars used within the geographical limits of the republic was F. X. Komarek of Vienna. He was a general engineer and boiler maker rather than a railway engine builder and also the builder of the only design of steam road wagon built in modern Austria.

The first railcars Komarek built were a series of three four wheelers for the 760mm gauge lines of the NÖLB, turned out in 1903. In them the leading axle was driven by outside cylinders placed under the body of the car between the axles, steamed by a vertical boiler. An austere match-board sided body with twenty-two seats was provided, having an open sided end platform. These cars were used on the Waldviertalbahn based on Gmund. About the same time (1903) the kk St. B bought a similar car, but with only sixteen seats, for use on the Triest-Parenzo line. A few years later this was transferred to the stock of the Pinzgauer Lokalbahn (Zell to Krimml). It was still there when the BBÖ took over and lasted until 1929 in contrast to its three contemporaries on the Waldviertalbahn which were scrapped between 1908 and 1911.

The NÖLB bought three further four wheeled Komarek cars in 1904, for use on the Mariazellerbahn from St. Pölten to Mank, basically resembling the 1903 examples but a little larger and fitted with four more seats. Finally, in 1906, the NÖLB bought five examples of an altogether larger and more developed car in which the rear end of the forty-four seater passenger compartment was carried on a bogie and the leading end was articulated onto a 2-4-0 vertical boilered locomotive unit. Two of these went to the Waldviertalbahn for working the line southward from Gmund to Gross Gerungs, one of which, in turn, was sold to the Steiermarkische Landesbahnen for use between Weiz and Birkfeld where it served from 1921 to 1926 (approximately).

Chapter VI
Locomotives between the wars

The situation in the Republic of Austria on the first day of its existence was precarious in the extreme. The deposed Emperor Karl was in retirement within the country at Eckartsau, declining exile, and had relinquished active rule but refused to abdicate. The administration headed by Karl Renner had as yet not been confirmed in power by a general election and its authority was contested on the one hand by a considerable body of royalists and on the other by a by no means negligible number of revolutionary Socialists and Communists. In addition bands of deserters from the demoralized army and small bodies of armed common criminals were at large in the countryside incapable of being held in check by what remained of the police force.

On the other hand, unlike the situation in 1945, the territories themselves had, on the whole, not suffered damage by bombardment or by battle though much of the country's industry had been worn out or depleted to serve the war effort and the railways, in particular, were in a run down state. On the first morning of Armistice and of the Republic it was difficult to know which locomotives and rolling stock would return to their home depots or even which crews would report for duty. Would, for instance, a German speaker from Prague elect to return there or to stay on in Vienna or would an official promoted from Galicia to head office want to remain at his post? The railway administration had, in the slightly longer term, moreover, no means of determining which locomotives would remain Austrian if and when a final settlement was reached on the division of the former kk St. B assets and had, in consequence, to fall back upon pragmatism as a means of carrying on, by using whatever was actually to hand. If a locomotive was there it was used. Deep mined coal, the main sources of which in old Austria had become Czech or Polish, was almost unobtainable, whilst brown coal, available nearer home, could not meet demand. Somehow, by using what stocks remained of hard coal, by eking out supplies of brown and by using wood where available some services were kept running through the autumn of 1918 and the winter of 1918/19.

Debate dragged on into 1921 as to the final division of rolling stock. Notes have already been given in Chapter III on the allocation or numerical division of some of the important classes and need not be repeated here. The results of this protracted negotiation were better than perhaps they might have been but as in all long haggles there were compromises and compromises produce anomalies. Thus though some classes changed hands en bloc or so as to leave substantial numbers in the hands of each new owning railway many of the classes taken over by Austria consisted of five engines or less. To instance an anomaly in another aspect, it may be related that the new state railways came into possession of one old 0-6-0 tender engine (Class 52) built in 1875 for the Istrianerbahn in Austria's former Adriatic territories and another (Class 94) from the Bukowinaer Lokalbahn, situated in what had, by 1921, become Rumanian territory. The BBO stock list of October, 1923 showed 38 classes containing five engines or less out of a total of 101 classes. By contrast, when the BBO rolling stock was given DRB numbers in 1938 the total of classes was 64 and, of these, 17 classes had either been acquired with the Sudbahn's Austrian assets in 1924 or built new since 1923. It is illuminating that of those sixty four classes taken over by the DRB only four classes (the BBO classes 170, 270, 378 and 80) reached or exceeded a hundred examples in each. The 80's were the Gölsdorf simple expansion two cylinder 0-10-0's, the 270's and 170's his single expansion and compound (respectively) 2-8-0's. The 378's were a BBO class and will be discussed in this chapter.

How Gölsdorf, had he lived, would have adapted to the condition which his successor, Johann Rihosek (1869–1956), had to face is an interesting speculation. It has been suggested that the two had worked together so long and were so agreed on policy that to study Rihosek is, virtually, to study Gölsdorf. This may be so but it is the author's conjecture that the latter would have had the greatest difficulty in cramping his outlook and style to dimensions where they might have been contained within the modest size and contracted resources of the Republic of Austria or of BBO. As early as 1917 Rihosek had published his ideas for a four-cylinder compound 2-8-4 with 1800mm driving wheels, essentially developing the 310's into an elongated version with a 16 tonne axle load, a proposal in which, it is said, he ran into opposition both specifically on the grounds of the proposed layout of the valve chests, the use of a cranked axle and the higher axle loading and in principle on the perpetuation of compounding. In any event such a proposal for a new class and even proposals for development of existing classes were ruled out by the course of events outlined in the opening paragraphs of this chapter.

Aside from locomotive matters the railway management had problems of their own in assessing the traffic requriements. Traffic into Vienna from the North and East, the traditional main directions of flow, was drastically curtailed both in passengers and goods. The Sudbahn routes to Italy and the new Yugoslavia were also affected but less severely whilst the former Cinderella, the western main-line from Vienna to Passau, Salzburg, Innsbruck and Switzerland was the only one to remain intact and of augmented importance. The development of new locomotive types was, however, given reduced priority in the higher planning echelons of the BBO by the ambitious decision to go for large scale electrification.

Accordingly the order for new express locomotives, when it came, was to St. EG for an updated version, designed by H. Steffan in the maker's drawing office, of the Sudbahn 570 class 4-8-0's originally the work of Karl Schlöss who had succeeded Prossy in control of the Sudbahn locomotive department. The most important change was the substitution of poppet valves for the original design of piston valve. First delivered in 1923 the class reached an eventual total of forty of which seven were lost, from various causes, in the second war but the thirty-three survivors of which remained intact until 1957 whereafter they were withdrawn, as a result of electrification, as they required major repairs until the last went ten years later. For some years they were used with the 310's on the western main line to Salzburg and Passau and also from Vienna to Villach over the Sudbahn line. They were, however, subject to a maximum permissible speed of 90k.p.h. an obstacle to improved train timings.

Rihosek has often been treated with less than justice by commentators. He had been in Gölsdorf's office since 1897 and was a world renowned expert on train braking particularly the vacuum brake. The circumstances in which he took office were extremely adverse – in the depths of a war from which, whether the Central Powers or the Allies had won, Austria seemed destined to emerge a loser either by domination by a victorious Germany or dismemberment, as came to pass, by the triumphant Allies. He had moreover long been aware, also, of the need to decrease rather than to augment the range of components required to keep the locomotive stock in repair and to standardise them as between locomotive types wherever possible. Thus his Class 270 two cylinder simple 2-8-0's of 1917 were a development of the existing Class 170's and it was not to be expected that in them he would throw overboard all the precepts to which he had hitherto subscribed nor that he would add to the diversity that, inherited from the constituent companies, was already the bane of his life. The first post monarchy building of locomotives was of 270's and throughout the life of BBÖ there was a stud of 100 of them. Moreover the Czechs, who had inherited the initial batch, also multiplied the class and this popularity was ultimately their undoing so far as Austria was concerned for of the hundred examples existing when the DRB took over in 1938 only a quarter came back into OBB hands.

The Class 81 2-10-0's, two cylinder simples with 590×632 cylinders, though not built until 1920, were designed in the closing phases of the war using the boiler of the existing 380 class compounds. A modification to a few examples in 1922 increased the superheater area from 40 to 73 square metres. Between 1920 and 1923 seventy-three were built at Wiener Neustadt. A compound version (the 181 Class) with two cylinders 620 and 870×632mm was a less happy design which ran to only 27 units, the last of which went for scrap in 1952.

Yet another example of Rihosek's aptitude for meeting fresh needs with existing components was his 82 Class in which design the boiler, engine and running gear of the large superheater 0-10-0 tender engines of Class 80.90, dating from 1911, was used as the basis of a 2-10-2 tank for heavy banking and shunting duties.

During this period the Sudbahn, with an undertaking now divided between three sovereign countries, was engaged in a struggle to maintain its very existence with a much reduced traffic. Its only post – 1918 construction was a group of six 0-10-0's of Class 480 turned out in 1921 for the Semmering. With two 610×632mm cylinders, a boiler pressure of 14 Atmospheres, 1258mm wheels, 3.80 square metres of grate area, 176 square metres of general heating surface and 45 square metres of superheater area they were rather more powerful than Gölsdorf superheated 0-10-0's of Class 80.900 but the class was never multiplied on the BBO after the absorption of the Subdahn's Austrian routes in 1924.

Rihosek found himself increasingly at odds with the BBÖ management over locomotive policy. Doubtless things were not helped in general by the political and financial instability of the country nor, in particular, by the heavy expense of the electrification programme. Despite these problems he made a determined start on the culling of minority classes, a policy continued by his successor. By 1925 he had eliminated thirteen classes. More positively he began the systematic use of feedwater heaters and the rebuilding with poppet valves of classes assigned a useful length of further service. In 1926, however, he retired from office prematurely and took the chair of locomotive design at the Vienna University of Technology. He was succeeded by Alexander Lehner (1886–1954). The last locomotives put in hand by Rihosek were a further batch of the 629 Class of superheated 4-6-2T originally designed for the Sudbahn in 1914, and built, with steel fireboxes, by the kk St. B from 1917 to 22. Yet a further batch with slightly increased water capacity was built under Lehner in 1927 (designated 629.500) bringing the class total to 85.

To enable the work, initiated by Rihosek, of clearing overage and minority classes to proceed Lehner commissioned from Floridsdorf the linked classes 378 of 2-8-2T's and 478 of 0-8-0T's, fifty of the latter and 167 of the former in which boiler, superheater, driving wheels, axles and engine parts were in common though the 478's had 530mm diameter cylinders where the 378's had 480, both having 570 stroke, a variation one would have expected in a locomotive intended for shunting and marshalling yard duties. The two classes enabled Lehner to sweep away a large number of worthy old veterans which had been retained for work on secondary lines. Both classes were provided with poppet valves which had been adopted as standard practice and this made them both quick and easy to reverse. It has been remarked that a 478 could carry out a shunting movement whilst the corresponding diesel was getting up its revs to do so.

In the meantime the electrification of the main line from the Swiss frontier over the Arlberg to Innsbruck and on to Salzburg had been proceeding with technical success but increasing concern at the cost. It was slowed because of the chronic fiscal malaise of the country so that the overhead did not reach Salzburg until 1929. The work was put in hand of improving the mainline east of Salzburg and from Wels to Passau by underline strengthening and by relaying but the scheme for extending electric working over these sections, conceived in the heady opening of the republic was seen to present grave problems in financing.

On the other hand this western main line had grown in traffic where all others had contracted and train weights of the order of 500/550 tonnes were being reached on the more important international trains with loads of 700 tonnes not unknown. Since the top train weight which the 310 Class 2-6-4's could handle over the route was about 450 tonnes whilst the 113 class 4-8-0's lacked climbing speed double heading was the order of the day and/or banking up to the easternmost summit at Rekawinkel in the Wienerwald and at the Salzburg end. The position was made worse by the top speed restriction of 90kph on the Class 113's which, by restricting speed on down-grades, cramped their overall speed performance.

Both these types had an axle loading of 15 tonnes to suit the old restrictions but with the proposed track improvements the limit was scheduled to be raised to 18 tonnes. As things stood the method of working was very wasteful with much double heading and the employment of bankers to start single headed trains from rest in stations disadvantageously situated on gradients. The worst of the gradients up to Rekawinkel and on the eastbound run from Salzburg through the Northern fringe of the Salzkammergut to Ederbauer were of the order of 1.0 to 1.1% uncompensated up which both the 310's and 113's could maintain 40kph with trains within their rated loadings.

The alternatives, therefore, were the effective but expensive electrification proposals or the building of a new class of steam locomotives capable both of taking at least a 530 tonne train single-handed up the ruling grades without dropping below 60kph and of speeds up to the permitted maximum of 100kph on more favourable stretches. It was to this latter question of how a steam alternative might be developed that Lehner addressed himself. With the new 18 tonne axle loading the available adhesive weight (54 tonnes) in a six-coupled engine of moderate driving wheel diameter would have been just sufficient for the purpose, given the requisite power output, and could, indeed, have handled 650 tonne loads on the so-called level sections. It would, however, have needed to be banked up to Rekawinkel and from Salzburg to Ederbauer whilst recovery from signal checks on adverse sections of the route would have been slow.

In March 1927, he began to discuss with Oscar Seidl, chief designer at Wiener Neustadt, the possibility of developing a successor class to the 310's, retaining the 2-6-4 arrangement which he liked because of the freedom it conferred on firebox size without taking the axle load on the carrying truck too high. These were to have been three cylinder simples with Heusinger valve gear and Lentz poppet valves. The discussions were based upon a sixteen ton axle loading which, though below the maximum to be permitted on routes for which they were being designed, would have given a great increase in route availability elsewhere.

65

The available extra axle loading was, however to be made use of on banks by a proposed system of transferring extra load onto the driving axles when additional adhesion was require.

News of these discussions reached the ears of Arno Demmer the President of Floridsdorf in March, 1927. The possibility of important Federal Railway work being placed with a rival concern without competitive tenders might well have moved him to action in any circumstances. In the murderously competitive conditions of 1927 it aroused him to a lightning campaign to circumvent what he believed might happen. He immediately entrusted his chief designer, Wilhelm Schindler, with the designs and Adolph Giesl Gieslingen with the calculations for a contrary proposal for an eight-coupled design proposed by the latter. For his part in order to forestall a possible fait accompli, Demmer secured an immediate meeting with Lehner's superior Werkstättendirektor Oskar Taussig at which he asked for and was granted an extension of time for the submission of counter proposals.

This did nothing to endear the Floridsdorf camp to Lehner but in order to understand his opposition to an eight-coupled design it is necessary to digress a little. Dr Basch, of the Wiener Neustadt Works, had secured his doctorate by a painstakingly researched thesis on the increase in resistance in coupled locomotives in relation to the number of coupled axles. In it he deduced, by faultless mathematics but, as it turned out, insufficient logic, that resistance increased with disproportionate sharpness in locomotives with more than three coupled axles. In arriving at his conclusions, however, he failed to introduce any factor to compensate for wheel diameter. In consequence he fell into the lapse of comparing the resistance of four coupled designs consisting in the main of mixed traffic or passenger locomotives with six-couplers spread over goods, mixed traffic and passenger and with eight-couplers dominated by heavy goods locomotives. As this fallacy had passed unremarked by the assessors of his thesis there are perhaps no grounds for excessive criticism of Lehner for allowing Basch's thesis to mould his views of eight coupled express locomotives. On the other hand, one ought not to withhold recognition of the perspicacity of Schindler and Giesl-Gieslingen in detecting the fallacy it contained and correcting it in their design. In his calculations the latter adopted a multiplier of 60% of Basch's figure but subsequent experience proved that 50% would have sufficed. Nor ought we to withhold credit from Demmer and the company who subsequently endorsed their conclusions by entering into binding performance guarantees based upon them.

Initially the proposition prepared by Floridsdorf utilised three cylinders but it was shortly supplemented by a proposal for a simpler and cheaper two cylinder design still capable of fulfilling the traffic requirements.

Some while before these events Giesl-Gieslingen had privately undertaken a traffic survey on the western main line between the Vienna Westbahnhoff and Rekawinkel which provided many of the facts he used in the preparation of the Floridsdorf documentation. In the analysis which Demmer presented to Taussig the point was made that in all-weather conditions the load limit of a six-coupled locomotive, even with 18 tonne axle loading, would have been 590 tonnes and to have achieved this this would have entailed some sacrifice of speed capability. Moreover, it was pointed out, even at the time of writing, 590 tonnes was barely sufficient and train loadings in excess of 600 tonnes were cropping up from time to time which would have overstretched the new six coupler which Lehner proposed, thereby reactivating the existing bug-bears of the cost and inconvenience of bankers to Rekawinkel and Ederbauer. It was further argued that the evidence was that train loadings would continue to increase. In this the reading of the future was astray for within less than four years the onset of the slump was drastically to reduce traffic.

It was calculated that the two cylinder eight-coupler would be capable not only of taking train weights of 660 tonnes using a 16 tonne axle loading on the driving wheels but 760 tonnes using the proposed 18 tonne axle loading. Again calculations were set out proving that such trains could be brought to Salzburg faster and at a reduced coal consumption because the capacity of the boiler was such there would be no need to thrash it.

This evidence from Floridsdorf, though by no stretch of the imagination to be considered as disinterested, posed a very considerable problem to Taussig. The issue was too important and the evidence too direct to be put aside yet Lehner, his own chief locomotive engineer, by his partisan upholding of the opposing view seemed disqualified from offering advice. He solved his dilemma by seeking an independent report from a well-respected Austrian locomotive engineer detached from the debate. Richard Schager on whom his choice fell had, until the amalgamation of 1924, been the Operating Superintendant of the Sudbahn and was a lecturer on railway materials and equipment at the Vienna University of Technology, a highly capable engineer and a man of integrity.

On 13th June, 1927 Wiener Neustadt submitted a counter proposal for a three cylinder 2-8-4 but this was, in effect, a side issue. The primary task of Schager's investigation was to deliver a considered evaluation of the relative merits of the 2-6-4 and 2-8-4 proposals. His conclusion was that the case for the eight coupler had been soberly stated, was established beyond doubt and merited being implemented. In consequence of his report both the three cylinder and two cylinder versions were put in hand, initially for 16 tonne axle loadings, but as progress with the track improvement programme was found to be going forward well the higher axle loading of 18 tonnes was finally adopted.

At first Lehner, perhaps piqued at having had his advice passed over, was somewhat less than enthusiastic about the matter but as the work of finalising the designs went on in discussions with Wiener Neustadt over the three cylinder and with Floridsdorf over the two cylinder the heat and excitement of launching a major new express locomotive reawakened his enthusiasm and soothed his feelings, a process assisted by the facts that little was known, other than to the parties involved, about the disagreement so that the question of face to the outside world was hardly involved and that the Floridsdorf camp displayed considerable tact in their dealings with him.

The designs were finalized by the respective makers using certain of the major elements interchangeably but there were differences in such items as the trailing trucks and the valve gear. The three cylinder design was given the class number 114 and the two cylinder 214. As the work of building the prototypes progressed Lehner seems to have become increasingly reconciled to the situation. By the time they had appeared and could be seen to be successful he had, to all intents and purposes, put behind him the difference surrounding their inception.

Indeed he may well have taken the view that disagreements inside the department were no business of the world at large. Lehner suffered from the disadvantage of living in the shadow of Gölsdorf, whose personal charisma he could not match and who had, moreover, worked in circumstances denied to Lehner, in whose term of office the steam locomotive lived more or less constantly under the threat of a notice to quit in favour of electrification, tolerated rather than desired in a country where the geographical, political and financial restraints were almost suffocating. If he is to be denied the extravagant praise he has been sometimes accorded he should perhaps be allowed in return the recognition of the circumstances in which he had to operate and credit for being a pragmatist.

Subsequent events justified, in some degree, his reservations on the use of eight coupled wheels though not his obstinacy. The splendid capabilities of the 214's were largely made unnecessary through the thirties by the reduction in train weights brought about by the slump and in the immediate post-war years by electrification.

The Floridsdorf prototype was ready for road testing in November and officially delivered early in December, 1928 but Wiener Neustadt who had perhaps the harder task took four months longer, not assisted by the harassing financial problems by which the firm was increasingly beset. The duo were designed for 120kph maximum speed (20% above the maximum permitted) but the 214 actually attained 156kph the highest speed recorded of any Austrian steam locomotive. They were put into service between Vienna and Passau and at once distinguished themselves by their performance. From dynamometer car records during the summer and autumn of 1929 service outputs of the order of 2500/2700 I.H.P. were recorded and the maximum noted was 2900 I.H.P. Whilst hauling the Arlberg Orient express on 19th February, 1929 No. 214.01 was in collision with the Orient Express at Tullnerbach-Pressbaum, suffering front end damage. Whilst this was being repaired the chance was taken to provide a Kyäla blast pipe modified to the suggestion of Dr Giesl-Gieslingen then still on the staff of Floridsdorf and this was standardised for future examples.

The trials of the two locomotive coincided with the onset of the slump which the following year settled the fate of all the Austrian locomotive builders except Floridsdorf who took over the designs and good-will of Wiener Neustadt, StEG and Krauss, Linz, a subject discussed later in the Chapter. Despite the financial problems the final phases of the track strengthening were complete by the end of 1931. A further six examples of Class 214 were ordered for delivery during the autumn of 1931 and a final six in 1936.

The decision to proceed with the 214 Class instead of the 114 Class represented financial commonsense. The 214 was master of the work for which it was intended and a less complicated design. It was not until after BBO had been merged into DRB that traffic recovered to the extent that the 214's were really being worked in the way they were designed for.

The 214's were doubly unfortunate in that the traffic for which they were designed had diminished before the first production batch was complete and also that they came a little too soon to profit by the refinements of boiler design which came with the thirties and which gave what was, as it turned out, the final polish to European steam express locomotive performance. Though they may thus have missed their optimum what they achieved was remarkable. Despite the fact that they filled the 4.65m Austrian loading gauge, had a two wheeled leading truck rather than a bogie and were a two cylinder design they gave a rock-steady ride with remarkable absence of hammer blow on the track, the result of the drive being onto the third coupled axle. It had been calculated by Giesl Gieslingen during the early stages of the proposal that to have driven onto the second axle would have led to fluctuations between 80 and 180% of the static axle load during each half a revolution when working hard i.e. five times a second at 60kph, the speed which the builders guaranteed the locomotive to maintain over Rekawinkel and up to Ederbauer. The use of the third axle halved these variations though at the expense of very long main rods (4.25m), of I – section nickel-manganese steel, probably the longest ever used.

Almost the only visible changes made in 114.01 and 214.01 were in the provision of smoke deflectors, found to be required during the first two months of working 214.01. At first small deflectors behind the chimney were tried, with no benefit, and long DRB type were then fitted, No. 114.01 coming out new with similar but shorter, deflectors.

Wilhelm Schindler and his design team were at particular pains to obviate the frame troubles which were by then becoming painfully apparent in the 380's. The plate frames were stiffened and boxed with a two piece steel casting running from the front buffer beam to before the fourth coupled axle. The class 214's suffered a number of derailments, mostly through driver error in passing through temporary speed restrictions without slackening speed (though one through the removal of a rail by saboteurs in the political troubles of 1934 and another in 1939, unfortunately with fatal consequences, at St. Valentin through the driver passing a poorly sited signal at danger) but in all these mishaps the frames proved resistant to distortion.

In between the two batches of 214's Lehner produced another class that, in an unassuming and traditional way, was also remarkable, the Class 729 4-6-4 tanks designed in 1931 with a 16 tonne axle loading and an all-up weight of 109 tonnes. In them he used 1614mm driving wheels (standard with the 429 and 629 Classes) but they were much larger and more powerful engines than a 629 (3.6 square metres of grate compared with 2.7 square metres, 171 square metres of fireside heating surface against 141 and 45 square metres of superheater surface against 29). During the lean years of the slump they often hauled the Arlberg and Orient expresses which had been much reduced in size. Later they were to be found on short distance fast and semi-fast trains around Vienna, particularly on the former Franz-Josef Bahn. Twenty-six were built, the last ten coming out after DRB had taken over and they survived intact until 1967 when the "Schnellbahn" developments in Vienna displaced them. Half were scrapped at once and the remainder all disappeared within the next five years.

Because of the high cost of working lightly trafficked lines by conventional methods in a manner brisk enough to retain traffic against road competition Lehner was asked to produce a class of light, fast locomotive that might provide a means of tackling the problem. Probably as an experiment he took two old Class 97 0-6-0T's, the original design of which dated from 1878, and rebuilt them (1934/35) as 2-2-2T, the former 930mm diameter driving wheels being replaced by 1450mm wheels, making them very much faster than before. Thus equipped they were, after trials to study their behaviour, set to work in Carinthia. One became a casualty of the war but the second lived to become Class 69 of the ÖBB and was not withdrawn until 1972, having been adapted for bridge testing by concentrating weight on the single driven axle so as to load the track with a force of 33 tonnes. Concluding, perhaps, that the solution he sought was not to be found without a more radical approach he put in hand a new class of very light locomotive combined with a luggage van, rather on the lines of those produced by Louis Gölsdorf and Elbel fifty years before. These took the form of small 2-4-2's designated DT1, with railed in running plates, reminiscent of Russian practice, the boilers having only 0.8 square metres of grate, and 46 square metres of general waterside heating surface but 21 square metres of superheater heating surface. The cylinders were 290×570mm, the driving wheels 1450mm. Their size can be judged from their total weight of only 45 tonnes. Twenty of the DT1's were built in all between 1935 and 1938. "DT" stood for Dampf Triebwagen" (steam railcar) and the possibility was considered when the class was built that the locomotive might be operated by one man, as the guard, who doubled up as conductor, was also based on the locomotive with access to and from the train by way of the railed in walkways. The idea of using them for light fast trains on main lines failed, as it had with Gölsdorf's fundamentally similar effort with the Class 112 in 1905/06, because of the inability of the system to respond to fluctuating demand. In consequence their usefulness came down mainly to limited stop services either on the suburban routes from Vienna or on the more important branches and to relieving diesel railcars on country branches. They were quite capable of working at speeds up to the permitted limit of 100kph and on test one of them exceeded 135kph, so that lokalbahnen hardly enabled them to show their paces.

Whilst the DT1's were being built Floridsdorf also produced a steam railcar of arresting design for the EWA which was by that time finding the need for economy pressing and was seeking a car for mainline work which could be driven by one man. The result was a design of considerable originality in which an oil fired vertical boiler was mounted in the centre of the car, which was carried on double bogies, one of which was the power unit. The three inside 250×300mm cylinders of the power bogie drove a counter shaft connected by rods to the driving axle. The power unit was thus a 0-4-0. The driving position was centrally at high level over the luggage/boiler compartment that formed the centre of the car. The front and rear saloons were joined by a side corridor alongside the boiler space. It is said to have been an uncanny experience to sit in the front of the car apparently proceeding without a driver. Soon afterwards the EWA was taken over by BBÖ and almost immediately by the DRB and the project was not followed up though the actual car did not disappear until the aftermath of the 1939/45 war. It is said that it was heavy on maintenance and this may well have been so. More to the point the BBÖ had already developed the VT 41, 42 and 44 diesel electric railcars of sturdy and useful designs which enjoyed up to forty years of active and untemperamental service which may have made the running authorities somewhat impatient of this steam prima donna.

Almost the last act performed by Lehner before the Anschluss in March, 1938 was the initiation of a new design of combined rack and adhesion locomotive, to be classified 369, for the Erzberg mineral trains. The new class was a 2-12-2 superheated tank engine weighing 125 tonnes capable of starting train weights of 400 tonnes up a 7.2% grade. Partly because of the upheavals which followed the change in control of the railways and partly because the rack rails required to be strengthened to deal with the full power of these locomotives the commencement of building was delayed and it was not until 1941 that the first two (and only) units were delivered. The rack strengthening was never completed and consequently the two giants never worked at full capacity. They were, in fact, the most powerful rack locomotives in service anywhere and it is a matter for regret that they became little more than white elephants.

At the beginning of 1924 the stock of standard gauge locomotives of the BBÖ and the lines it was responsible for operating amounted to 2427. By the end of 1937 it had declined to 1834 of which an unspecified number were stored in or near working order in the hope that a traffic revival would necessitate their reinstatement in active service. The terminal in Vienna of the former Nord West Bahn (reduced after 1918 to a short suburban line and a country branch) had been taken out of use by transferring its trains to the Franz Josef station and the main hall was brought into use as a repository for locomotives temporarily withdrawn. Lesser numbers were kept at locomotive sheds. The western electrification programme from Switzerland to Salzburg and to the Brenner was completed, rather later than intended, in

1930, coinciding with the slump. At the end of 1929, 2434 locomotives were in service or reserve. By December 1930 there were only 2173, a decline at the rate of over twenty per month during the intervening period. The locomotive department found itself, therefore, more or less constantly in surplus in locomotive numbers whilst financially the tendency was remorselessly towards deficit.

The combination of these two circumstances inevitably meant that the inauguration of new locomotive types was not encouraged but rather making do with what already existed. Some interesting rebuildings took place during the 1920's, Gölsdorf's least successful design, the four cylinder compound 2-8-2 passenger locomotives of Class 470 in which the merits of his first two four cylinder designs (Classes 108 and 110) were sacrificed by the use of combined piston valves for the high and low pressure cylinders each side (in lieu of separate valve gear to each cylinder) had suffered a good deal of punishment through wartime hard work and neglect. They were, moreover, unpopular on account of their reputation as fireman killers. By 1926 some action was called for. Rihosek, who may have had a hand in the design, had foreborne to interfere with them but when Lehner took over he commenced to deal with the class, scrapping the examples which were in too poor a condition to justify rebuilding and reconstructing the remainder as two cylinder simples with poppet valves. Eight were thus dealt with between 1926 and 1928 being classified 670. One was lost in the war and the surviving seven ran intact until 1953 whereafter they were withdrawn in stages until the last was cut up in 1957.

Another interesting rebuild was the old Class 9 compound 4-6-0's dating from 1898, probably Gölsdorfs most uncomely design and his only locomotives of that wheel arrangement. In 1924 a beginning was made of rebuilding them as simples with poppet valves, the boilers being superheated at the same time. Little changed in their external appearance but their performance was enhanced whilst maintenance was decreased. Nineteen were rebuilt, of which eleven survived to become DRB property and the last was not cut up until the late forties.

The building and rebuilding of locomotives with poppet valves generally made use of Lentz valves operated by oscillating cam actuated by Heusinger valve gear. The exceptions to this general rule were the five 629 class tanks (629. 500–504) built by Krauss Linz in 1927 in which Caprotti valve gear was used, probably to check whether or not the advantages were sufficient to justify the royalties due under the patent. Since the original form of Caprotti gear had constant compression and release no increase in efficiency resulted against the newer form of the Lentz gear and these engines received Lentz gear in the mid-thirties.

Once the arrears of major repairs had been carried out in the opening days of the Republic it became apparent that the amount of work available to the four locomotive building works in Austria was insufficient and despite efforts to allocate the available orders on a rational basis through the Osterreichische Eisenhahn – Verkehrs Anstalt of which all were members the position of the four deteriorated, though Floridsdorf, headed by the dynamic Arno Demmer, fared better than the other three. Krauss, Linz, for instance, which severed the connection with the parent in 1920, built only 351 locomotives in the succeeding decade. Amongst the innovations introduced by Demmer to combat the fall in orders was the building of steam rollers and, later, diesel rollers. The onset of the slump gave the lie to any hopes that might have been entertained as to recovery and in 1930 Floridsdorf absorbed the three competing works, in part by payment in shares and in part by cash. In the case of Krauss, the smallest, 1.65 million schillings were in shares and 1.2 million in cash. All the works, except Floridsdorf, were closed and dismantled, though Demmer was able to keep the best of the machine tools and the ablest of the staff and foremen.

On the 760mm gauge lines relative to their route mileages the twenties saw a considerable amount of locomotive building. The opening of the new line from Ruprechtshofen to Gresten prompted the BBÖ to place orders with Krauss for three 0-8-2 side tanks of Class P (originally designed for the Triest-Parenzo line in 1911). These three further examples were delivered in 1926.

In 1928 the BBÖ ordered from Krauss the first of a new design of superheated 0-6-2T – an updated version of Class U, designated Uh – the first two of which were delivered in 1928. Three more followed in 1929, and a sixth in 1930. At this point the Krauss, Linz works lost its separate identity to Floridsdorf who delivered the two final Uh's in 1931. The Uh was a formidable machine for its gauge weighing 28.1 tonnes all up with 1.06 square metres of grate and 44 square metres of heating surface and Caprotti valve gear *. No Uh01 went to Waidhofen on the Ybbstalbahn to replace the 1898 Krauss 0-6-2 which had been transferred to the Triest-Parenzo line in 1918 and lost to Italy. Uh 02 and 03 went to the Bregenzerwaldbahn to replace U26 and U36 left in Russia and Jugoslavia respectively whilst Uh 04, 05 and 06 went to Zell-am-See for use on the line to Krimml. The last two, Uh 101 and 102, went to Zell and Obergrafendorf respectively. Another of the same type was built in 1930 by Krauss for the Zillertalbahn on which it was No. 5. This was rebuilt in 1941 from Caprotti to Lentz valve gear. It carried the works number 1521 and was the last locomotive sent out from Linz.

The 760mm lokalbahn from Kühnsdorf (on the standard gauge line from Klagenfurt to Bleiburg) to Eisenkappel, hitherto a very lightly trafficked line, had been worked from the opening by two small 0-6-2T of the T class, one of which was ceded to Jugoslavia in 1918. In 1924 to deal with a developing traffic in timber the BBÖ obtained a powerful ten coupled superheated tank in which the leading four axles were carried in inside frames and the final axle in outer frames with liberal provision for lateral movement, on the Klien Lindner system developed in Saxony.

A similar locomotive was delivered in 1926 for use on the Murtalbahn (owned by the Steiermarkische Landesbahnen) and a third, for the same owners for use on the newly opened and steeply graded line from Birkfeld to Ratten. This final example had Caprotti valve gear.

Two other ten couplers, side tank engines by Maffei of Munich dating from 1920 were used on 760mm lines in Austria, the first (Works No. 3965) on the Salzkammergut Lokalbahn, the second (No. 3966) on Birkfeld-Ratten line.

*The two Floridsdorfers had Lentz poppet valve gear.

Chapter VII
The War and the concluding years of steam

The change that confronted BBÖ personnel on the day of the Anschluss, though it is doubtful if anyone realised it at the time, was the termination of the process of development of the Austrian steam locomotive which had thereto been continuous for some ninety five years. Drastically though the system had been pruned by the breaking up of the old imperial and royal empire in 1918 the central organisation had remained, with the same chief locomotive engineer in office and continuity of designs and methods.

It is true that classes such as the DT1's in production in March 1938 were completed and the Class 389 (originally 269) 2-12-2 tanks for the Erzberg, which Lehner had on the drawing board at the time, were actually built in 1941 but the separate and distinct Austrian locomotive policy died in March, 1938. Oppressive as Austrians soon found the new regime to be in the political field the DRB, as the new masters of the Austrian railways from 18th March, were by no means stifling in the technical sense. Changes of policy in day to day matters were relatively few. The old divisions of the Federal Railways, Innsbruck, Linz, Villach and Vienna were maintained and the head office administration was kept, at least for the time being, as a sectional administration, with curtailed powers of decision, having to defer on major policy to the Ministry of Transport in Berlin, headed by Dr J. Dorpmuller, who was also General Manager of the DRB and on technical affairs to the Reichbahn Zentralamt.

Except for the old BBÖ classes 4, 92 and 94 each down to a solitary example and marked for scrapping each item of the locomotive stock was allocated a new number in the DRB series. The seventeen locomotives taken over from the Aspangbahn went straight from their old Aspang numbers to DRB numbers without carrying a BBÖ classification intermediately.

Though the DRB did not interfere with the running of Austrian locomotives on their native terrain none of the classes were numerous enough to be adopted as a DRB standard. This is not to say that they did not perform as well as or, in some cases, better than their German counterparts. Had a good Austrian class both outshone and out numbered a corresponding German class there might have been the possibility, human bias apart, of its being assimilated as a standard. As things stood there was no chance, with one exception, namely the 214's.

The 214's had become something of a legend with their towering bulk, easy riding, brisk and staccato starts with exchange traffic from Passau and the apparent ease with which they were able to lift a 700 tonne train to Rekawinkel summit almost at the end of the run from Passau to Vienna. The DRB seem to have determined to find out what they had acquired by way of fact as well as by way of legend. In March, 1939 No. 214-011, by then renumbered 12.011 on the DRB scheme, was taken to Germany for trials at Grunewald where it was tested by the Nordmann method using a dynamometer car with two braking locomotives behind it. The routes selected were the Potsdam – Magdeburg line and part of the Spandau-Hamburg route as far as Hagenow Land. A return trip in revenue service between Berlin and Breslau was marred by the blowing of a fusible plug which had been filled by accident with lead in lieu of the standard alloy. For reasons not recorded the firebar spacing was altered from 21mm to 28mm, perhaps to give better air space but in the event it led to appreciable quantities of fuel finding its way unburned into the ash pan.

The table below gives the conclusions reached.

Constant evaporation (DRB standard) 57 kg/square metre of total fireside heating surface per hour. Calorific value of fuel not stated but probably about 11000 BTU/lb.

Speed k.p.h.	d.b.h.p.	Coal consumption
60	1635	3.17
80	1556	3.31
100	1475	3.54

The average superheat temperature was 355 degrees C.

The test results seem to have left the Germans non-committal as to the 214's. Certainly there was never any question of their numbers being added to. How DRB policy would have manifested itself in Austria had peace continued is almost pointless conjecture for, by the Spring of 1939 having assimilated Czechoslovakia, the Reich was probably already committed to a policy of war on its eastern frontiers.

By 1938 the DRB had already introduced the prototype Class 50 2-10-0's in which the 20 tonne axle loading of the standard Class 44 2-10-0's had been brought down to 15 tonnes, clearly with an eye to increased route availability in the event of war. Though these locomotives were simplified by peace-time standards the demands of war once it had begun, made even further economies of labour and material necessary and led to the *Kriegsloks,* of Class 52 and later the heavier Class 42. Floridsdorf had some hand in the Class 50 programme and in building Classes 44 and 86 but it was in the production of Classes 42 and 52 of which 266 and 1168 examples respectively were built as main contractors plus work as sub-contractors that the works had its last fling on steam locomotives. Production of Class 42 continued until after 1945.

Relating these events, however, has distorted the chronological sequence of the narrative. One important pre-war decision remains to be noted. The use of the vacuum brake had been standard on the Federal Railways and the kk St. B before them and Austria had been a leading force, through Rihosek, on the railway side and the ex-patriate John Hardy and his Austrian born sons on the manufacturing side, in the development of automatic vacuum brake practice. Indeed some aspects of Austrian usage were peculiarly Austrian notably to apply the train brakes before the locomotive brakes, for which purpose locomotives were fitted with a combination valve. Because of the Austrian terrain locomotive tyres came under heavy wear and the use of the train tyres to take the initial braking load relieved the locomotive tyres of one element of wear. It also had the secondary benefit of preventing bunching of the train, keeping couplings tight and preventing snatching.

The DRB, by contrast, had air brakes as standard and the decision was taken to re-equip the former BBÖ stock with air brakes so as to conform. The war, however, had been fought and lost before the changeover was complete and the concluding stages were carried out by the post-war Austrian administration.

The effects of the war were too profound to be capable of summary in a few paragraphs. They happened broadly under three heads 1) changes brought about by general restrictions 2) changes caused by traffic directly related to the war 3) the effects of Allied action, particularly bombing.

Under the first heading may be classified a great variety of traffic changes in common with, say, Britain. The use of private cars was restricted almost to the point of extinction and bus mileages were curtailed to save liquid fuel. Troops travelled on leave, war-workers travelled to factories, local or short distance deliveries were increasingly made – by train. These increased the traffic and hence locomotive requirements on local lines.

During the first two years of the war traffic changes under the second heading came mainly into the category of increased mineral traffic – coal and iron ore in particular – troop movements and movement of finished products from armament factories. The occupation of Yugoslavia and Greece, the involvement of Hungary, Bulgaria and Rumania in the war, the advance into Russia and the tangled Italian situation made the second phase from mid 1941 very different. Traffic to and from the East restored the main lines intersecting Lower Austria to something approaching their pre 1914 importance whilst the old Sudbahn lines were also called upon to carry traffic such as they had not seen for years. The line from Vienna to Maribor via Graz, in particular, underwent a programme of bridge strengthening and re-routing which allowed more flexibility in axle loadings.

During this second phase the Allies increased their control of the air. Klagenfurt, Wiener Neustadt and St. Pölten, all junctions possessed of war factories, were bombed heavily. The balance of air power changed progressively in favour of the Allies to the extent that in the concluding months of the war it was difficult for a train to move on a main line in daytime without the danger of its being strafed.

The DRB administration brought in a number of ex-Prussian locomotives, some from Prussia itself, others "repossesed" from railways which had acquired them as reparations after 1918. Thus there were S10.1's, P4.2's, P10's, P8's, G8's, G8.1's G8.2's, G10's, T9.3's and T14's. It also imported some smaller Bavarian locomotives. There were a limited number of the new DRB 44 and 50 classes, a considerable number of 42's and something in excess of three hundred 52's as the latter two classes became available. Besides all these there were odd examples of Polish, French and Italian classes. Sundry Austrian locomotives, in turn, were taken away for use elsewhere.

When the dust had settled down after the surrender of 1945 the Russians controlled Vienna and much of Lower Austria, halted only by meeting American and British advances from the West and South. Traffic between the occupation zones was halted by political or military considerations but even where these did not apply the state of the track and rolling stock had an equally inhibiting effect.

On 27th April 1945, the lines which had belonged to the BBÖ before the Anschluss were reconstituted as the Österreichische Staatseisenbahnen (Austrian State Railways). Floridsdorf completed a batch of the Class 42 Kreigsloks which were in hand, the only steam locomotives built post-war for use in Austria, the United States contributed both their 2-8-0 tender locomotive and also the 0-6-0T's and the British found a number of military locomotives for use on Austrian lines. These supplementary locomotives taken with those existing locomotives still in working order or capable of early repair enabled services to be resumed on a limited but increasing scale.

The Österreichische Staatseisenbahn (Ö St. B) lasted only until 1947 when, on 5th August, the present regime, Österreichische Bundesbahnen, was established. By that time the quadripartite occupation had been settled onto a working basis with administration back in Austrian hands and the occupation troops forming a mainly military presence, frequently in very cordial relations with the resident population. The twenty-eight months of the State

Railway had seen off most of the pressing problems of repair and reinstatement of rolling stock and locomotives, track and signalling but much remained to be done with buildings, particularly the large termini in Vienna.

Fuel supplies were extremely problematical. Considerable quantities of locomotive coal were sent from America via Triest, much of it fairly poor stuff to begin with, and multiple handling reduced it to very small sizes. The dependence on this coal source and its shortcomings caused the Russian occupation administrators to order Ö.St. B to convert 200 locomotives to oil fuel. Doubtless politics had a hand in this also. As a result a start was made on conversions using either Swoboda or Hardy burners. These needed a small coal fire or a bed of slag over the grate and an appreciable amount of steam was consumed in atomising the fuel. Moreover they were noisy in operation producing an unpleasant droning roar.

During the Autumn of 1946 a Class 52 destined for use in Austria was brought back from Italy where the American railway corps had converted it to oil firing using a flat burner on the throat sheet with the oil coming through the upper nozzle and the steam through the lower, the grate being replaced by a trough lined with firebrick, holes through which provided the air, supplemented and regulated by a duct which replaced the firehold door. Whereas the earlier conversions had required the burners to be inserted in holes through the inner and outer backplates of the firebox the American method, improvised by an ingenious field workshop, needed no structural alterations. Moreover it was quieter, gave a better flame path, with a more even distribution of heat over the firebox plates and used less steam. Not surprisingly the Austrians adopted it.

The conversion programme, using Rumanian oil instead of American coal, was technically and financially successful but defeated by the failure of the Russians to ensure that supplies of oil arrived regularly. The railway dragged its feet over the conversion programme and it petered out before even the initial 200 units were converted. Supplies of Bohemian and Silesian locomotive coal became available again and oil firing became a dead issue. The electrification programme was revived with great vigour in 1946, as narrated in Chapter II, linked with the phasing out of steam.

After the electricification of the western main line had reached Vienna in 1952, displacing the Class 214 2-8-4's four of them (by then 12.01, 12.03, 12.08 and 12.11 under the ÖBB numbering scheme) were transferred to Vienna Sud depot for working over the Semmering and into Carinthia. Later they were joined by 12.10 and this latter performed the last steam working on the line on 23rd September, 1956, incidentally the last run performed in revenue earning service by one of the class.

The locomotive fuel situation in the first five years after the war led to a final notable Austrian contribution to locomotive engineering. Poor performance by locomotives fired on very broken or weathered coal came from the inability to burn enough of it to produce the required amount of heat, primarily because enough air could not penetrate the fire bed. Widening the spacing of the firebars was no answer because of losses into the ash pan whilst sharpening the blast by contracting the nozzle(s) led to back pressure and caused trouble by taking fines more or less from the fireman's shovel straight through the tubes. Fine coal was also lifted from the fire bed and led to lineside fires in dry weather.

In 1951 Dr Giesl Gieslingen, whom we noted earlier as involved in the design of the 214 class at Floridsdorf, revealed his design for the ejector which has since borne his name, designed to take the place of the blast arrangement in use up to that time. By his arrangement of oblong chimney and seven fan-like jets a continuous effect of reduced exhaust pressure was obtained resulting in distinctly lower back pressure on the pistons, in more even distribution of air through the firebed and in reduced disturbance of the incandescent fuel. Something in excess of two and a half thousand units were installed world wide, 452 of them on ÖBB locomotives intended to work after 1966.

Another invention by Dr Giesl Gieslingen was the micro-spark arrester of 1954 which helped to prolong the use of steam in Austria by reducing the lineside fires which had been the source of much popular criticism of steam traction. The last development of all was superheat boost in 1955.

By 1955 mainline steam haulage generally was within a year or so of extinction leaving the working of the old Franz Josef main line to the Czech frontier, freight and a limited number of local passenger workings on branch-lines as the scene of future steam activity. When the DRB had taken over the old BBO locomotive stud in March 1938 the total had stood barely over 1800. In 1946, by contrast, what the O.St. B took back was a rag-bag of 2786 locomotives but these were rapidly whittled down to 1982 in 1948 and 1647 at the end of 1952. By December 1956 the total was down to 1262, dropping about 9% per annum until by the end of 1960 it was 939. Of this total of 939 the make up was as follows.

Classes with ten or more examples in each

BBÖ Class	ÖBB	Total	Wheel arrangement
214	12	13	2-8-4 (in store)
113	33	22	4-8-0
429	35	26	2-6-2
-	42	15	2-10-0
-	50	12	2-10-0
-	52	204	2-10-0
-	152	36	2-10-0
270	156	15	2-8-0
80.90	57	32	0-10-0
-	657	58	0-10-0 (Prussian G10)
DT.1	3071	17	2-4-2T
629	77(2)	76	4-6-2T
729	78	26	4-6-4T
-	86	27	2-8-2 ex DRB
178	92	41	0-8-0T
478	392	43	0-8-0T
378	93	128	2-8-2T
82	95	22	2-6-2T
269	97	14	0-6-2T Rack
99	91	13	2-6-0
-	989 (1,2)	10	0-6-0T U.S.A.

Five of the ubiquitous Prussian P8's remained in service in 1960 as ÖBB Class 638 but all were gone by the end of 1966.

A survey of classes ten years later disclosed heavy casualties. Out of 350 standard gauge locomotives in use in December 1970 185 were Kriegsloks of the plate framed 52 and bar-framed 152 classes. Five of the Class 50 2-10-0's remained, thirty-two out of the 76 examples of the 629's (ÖBB 77.2) and only six of the 729's. The nimble and useful 378 class (ÖBB 93) still accounted for 91. Progressive withdrawals over the next three years brought steam locomotive classes down to the Class 52's, a few surviving 629's, forty three Class 93's and ten examples of the Erzberg rack 0-6-2T's of Class 69, together with the three 0-12-0T's of Class 269 on the same line. Apart from the Erzberg operation which, as to freight, was still 100% steam worked freight working by steam was restricted to Linz (mainly on the line North to Summerau), Vienna Nord (for working freight over the old Franz Josef Bahn and the other non-electrified lines) and Bruck a.d. Mur. The old NÖLB and other lines in the deep rurality of the Mistelbach area still had steam on passenger trains, mostly worked by 2-8-2T of ÖBB Class 93. All were intended to be superseded not later than the end of 1976 and the programme would, indeed, have gone as intended had it not been for the accident on the Erzberg during the replacement of steam rack by diesel adhesion working resulting in a runaway and derailment on the South side of the summit.

Operation by steam was continued whilst the braking situation was reviewed under the anxious eyes of the railway union, to prevent a recurrence. Satisfactory working procedures having been agreed, steam was finally withdrawn in 1977.

In the same year active steam working came to an end on the Graz-Köflacher Bahn, operating lines to the West of Graz. It will be recalled that the route runs west from Graz to a junction at Lieboch from which one line continues northward to Köflach where it serves the large opencast mine producing brown coal and southward to Wies-Eibiswald near the Yugoslav frontier. Both these lines carry passenger traffic worked, except at morning and evening peaks, by diesel railcars. The railway also operates the goods only Sulmtalbahn (opened in 1907). Though independent of the ÖBB it has been owned since 1924 by the Alpine-Montangesellschaft, the nationalized mining and steel company. Freight working in the period now under review was carried on until the sixties mostly by sixteen Gölsdorf compound 2-8-0's of ÖBB class 56 (BBÖ 170), of which one now remains in serviceable order. As the fireboxes of these locomotives wore out they were replaced by Class 52's and 152's which carried on steam working until the winter of 1977/78 during which a changeover was made to diesel working, though certain units of Class 52 are retained in reserve in working order and have boiler certificates valid until 1985.

The GKB also owned a 0-6-0 tender locomotive of the former Sudbahn Class 29, No. 680, built in 1860 as one of the first of its class. Because of its suitability for various lightly laid and awkwardly curved industrial connections of the GKB this remained in service long after its fellows had been withdrawn on the Federal Railways. During 1977 this locomotive was given a general repair in the GKB shops at Graz and is now in service for steam specials.

The only standard gauge public railway in Austria on which steam can be seen in revenue earning service at the time of writing (1981) is the Raab-Odenburg-Ebenfurter, with lines in both Hungary and Austria which has the interesting situation of being a privately owned Hungarian company, a polite fiction to cover its anomalous situation. Passenger working on this railway (commonly known as Gysev, from the initials of its Hungarian anme) is worked by Hungarian diesel railcars of varying vintages but steam, mostly Hungarian Class 376 2-6-0 tank engines, continues to appear at intervals on permanent way trains and the occasional freight working. In realistic terms, however steam working can be said to have ended.

On the 760mm gauge lines the picture is, however rather different. It was noted in the preceding chapter how steam locomotive building for the 760mm gauge ceased in 1931.

Subsequently a beginning was made in 1934 with the introduction of diesel electric locomotives when Simmering supplied two small four wheeled locomotives for the Ruprectshofen to Gresten line, followed by a third in 1936. Also in 1936 seven four axle diesel electrics were built using the same power unit as the successful VT42 class standard gauge railcars.

Here, however, as elsewhere the aftermath of the war produced changes such as few could have expected. The German Army had five classes of 750mm gauge locomotives, 0-4-0T and 0-6-0T designs, 0-6-0T's and 0-8-0T's with side tanks and a separate tender and 0-8-0T's. The Austrian railway authorities secured one of the 0-4-0's, built by Henschel in 1941 which was used mostly in the yard at St. Pölten Alpenbahnhof and one of the 0-6-0T's by the same builder and again dating from 1941. Four of the 0-6-0 tanks with tenders were acquired, the earliest by Henschel (1941) and the latter three, differing in points of detail, by Jung (1944), whilst they had three of the 0-8-0 version turned out by Franco-Belge in 1944. The list of acquisitions was topped off by four of the 0-8-0T's, by Franco-Belge (1944). Along with them they also acquired a 0-6-2 side tank by Krauss, Munich, originally built in 1920 for the Kreis Kreuznacher Kleinbahn in Germany. This was one of the longest lived of the batch, lasting until 1973, along with the 0-8-0T's with or without tenders. The single 0-4-0 ran until 1969, as did the 0-6-0T plus tender from Henschel but the three by Jung were cut up in 1956. All were regauged to 760mm.

A broadly similar ten coupled version of the tender/tank locomotives built by Borsig in 1939, went to the Salzkammergut Lokalbahn in 1945 together with, in 1946, a 0-8-0 (by Franco-Belge 1944) and, in 1945, two 0-6-0 (by BMF and Henschel respectively in 1942). The SKGLB also bought two Orenstein & Koppel 0-6-0T built in 1942. Though all these locomotives were of very basic wartime material they were a valuable supplement to the ageing locomotive stud of the SKGLB. The Borsig ten coupler went to the Zillertalbahn after the SKGLB closed in 1957. Since 1974 it has been on the Bregenzerwaldbahn of the ÖBB in the Vorarlberg.

The Steiermarkische Landesbahn also had three of the 0-6-0 tank plus tender locomotives (one by BMF, two by Jung) and one of the Franco-Belge 0-8-0T, previously on the SKGLB, all dating from 1944. The latter was rebuilt after purchase and was sold in 1969 to the Welshpool and Llanfair Light Railway on which it carries the name SIR DREFALDWYN.

Chapter VIII
Comments and Conclusions

The convenient identification of locomotives has been a problem that has exercised the ingenuity of railway managements since the beginning of steam traction. The method inherited from the horse-people was that of bestowing a name – of, so to speak, personalising each locomotive – and, soon afterwards, of developing this theme by giving locomotives of the same type, class names selected so as to be recognizably in the same category. Greek mythology was a fruitful source of names. So also was topography – names of rivers, cities, mountains, seas and oceans, lakes or countries. Prominent persons provided another found of inspiration so that locomotives received the names of men (and rarely, but sometimes, women) prominent in the theatre, arts, music, medicine, military or naval affairs, science or like categories. When the total locomotive stock of a railway was small and staff often illiterate or innumerate the system has some merit. Names are more vivid than numbers and it was easy for a railwayman to remember, say, that *Blucher* and *Wellington* were both generals of renown and that the two locomotives bearing their respective names belonged, therefore to the "General" class. Complications, as ever, soon ensued. If the (imaginary) railway cited above had also had a "Duke" class would the perplexed staff have assigned *Wellington* to the "Generals" or to the "Dukes"?

The KFNB alone, of the railways we are considering, originally used identification by name only. From 1837 to 1841 its engines had no running numbers or class numbers. By 1841 the method had become far too cumbersome even on that limited scale and though naming continued book numbers were assigned gradually both to classes and to individual machines within them. Other railways in metropolitan Austria used class titles and running numbers from their inception but without uniformity of system between the several railways and often without much logic within each system. Thus the Franz Josef Bahn used only running numbers, allocated in blocks to the classes. The Kaiserin Elizabeth Bahn used Roman numerals for classes and Arabic for running numbers with lower case letters to indicate sub-classes, a method also adopted on the Kronprinz Rudolf Bahn but whereas a Class II locomotive on the former was a 2-4-0 on the latter it was a 0-6-0. The Sudbahn used Arabic numerals for both classes and running numbers and eventually adopted the state railways system after it had been revised in 1904.

When the state began the nationalising of independent railways in 1882 a combination of capital letters and Roman numerals was used for classes, the primary significance of the letters being:

     A = Passenger locomotives
     B = Freight locomotives
     S = Secondary locomotives
     V = Shunting locomotives

These primary letters alone were applied only to the classes taken over from the Kaiserin Elizabeth Bahn. The locomotives of all other companies absorbed were given an identification letter which became part of the locomotive class titles. Thus Vorarlberger Bahn passenger locomotives became AVI and AVII, those from ·the Kaiser Franz Josef-Bahn became AFI and so on. For some curious reason the small 0-6-0T locomotives taken over from the Fehring-Furstenfeld line became Class F, with no primary letter.

With the beginning of the new kk St. B administration in 1884 a new system was devised and implemented in 1886 into which it was hoped it would be possible to introduce additional ranges of numbers for the locomotives acquired as further railways were added to the state fold. Furthermore the number system, by linking the number of the class with the running number, was calculated to provide information about the locomotive as well as its bare running number. Each locomotive carried a three or four digit number consisting of the class number plus a two digit running number within the class. Thus 901 was the first of Class 9. The classification of classes was as follows:

1 to 9	express locomotives
10 to 29	passenger locomotives
30 to 68	six-coupled freight locomotives
69	rack locomotives
70 to 79	eight-coupled freight locomotives
80 to 89	four-coupled branch line locomotives
90 to 99	six-coupled branch line locomotives

So long as the number of locomotives in a class did not exceed 99 this method worked without excessive pain but where the class totals topped the hundred confusion resulted, firstly because the next class number, if available, had to be taken to continue the class so that one class then had two class numbers and, secondly, because when this was done it produced a shortage of class numbers.

Because of these imperfections the system was changed again in 1904. The method instituted at that time was the work of Johann Rihosek then Karl Göldorf's right-hand man. Ever a pragmatist, Rihosek devised a new system that could straighten out the defects of the old with the minimum of fuss and renumbering. By his method a dot or decimal point separated the class number from the running number, getting rid of one of the major troubles of the previous classification. He then allocated class numbers on the following basis:

1 to 30	passenger locomotives
31 to 67	six-coupled freight locomotives
68 and 69	rack locomotives
70 to 79	eight-coupled freight locomotives
80 to 82	ten-coupled freight locomotives
83 to 89	light four-coupled locomotives
90 to 99	light six-coupled locomotives
100	twelve-coupled locomotives

To indicate a sub-class or rebuild a prefix number was used, so that a locomotive of Class 106 was a modified version of a Class 6 but this principle was varied from about 1907 onwards by using a sub-class number immediately after the decimal point and attached to the running number.

A few years of use showed that the numbers allocated to passenger classes were insufficient to make for entirely logical working. Thus, when Gölsdorf built his four cylinder compound 2-10-0's for passenger service he called them Class 280 – right for the number of coupled wheels but wrong in the service classification (freight) and wrong again in that, by logic, it made them a sub-class of the 180 class of 0-10-0 freight engines. Nevertheless, despite these shortcomings of logic, by the application of a certain amount of common-sense the method worked quite satisfactorily.

Tenders were always numbered separately. Classes 1 to 9 were for four wheelers, 10 to 79 for six wheelers and 80 to 99 for eight wheelers.

As has been noted the Sudbahn worked closely with the state system of 1904, an arrangement assisted in the respective locomotive departments by their being controlled at the relevant time by the Gölsdorfs, senior and junior, Louis and Karl. The class numbers used on the Sudbahn agreed with, or did not conflict with, those of the kk St. B classes.

This kk St. B method of numbering continued when the kk St. B became the BBÖ after 1918 and would probably have continued until steam came to an end had not the period of German rule intervened during which all locomotives and rolling stock were reclassified within the DRB system.

DRB practice used a category number of two digits followed by two digits denoting the class after which came the running number within the class. After the war ÖBB continued the DRB classification but reintroduced the dot between the class and running numbers. These are the class divisions in current use.

0 to 39	– passenger tender engines
40 to 59	– freight tender engines
60 to 79	– passenger tank engines
80 to 96	– freight and mixed traffic tanks
97	– standard gauge rack locomotives
98 and 99	– narrow gauge locomotives

Before 1938 narrow gauge locomotives had had a classification of their own consisting of a capital letter, usually that of the line for which they were first designed, followed by a lower case letter to indicate characteristics viz.

v for compound	(v = verbund)
h for superheated	(h = heissdampf)
z for rack equipment	(z = zahnrad)

All the steam locomotives in current use by ÖBB fall into classes 98 and 99. They remain in use for commercial reasons only viz. i) on the Waldviertalbahn and Steyrtalbahn no replacements have yet been provided, a subject we will revert to in a moment ii) on the rack lines respectively to the Schneeberg and Schafberg summits and to a limited extent on the 760mm Brengenzerwaldbahn steam working remains because it is an attraction to tourist traffic with the added incentive in the case of the rack lines that diesel replacements would have a high capital cost and be basically under used. Steam remains on the Steyrtalbahn because the actual railway is threatened by a road scheme and ÖBB have not been prepared to embark upon a replacement programme for a line thus under threat. The Waldviertalbahn runs in chilling proximity to the Iron Curtain in an area of sparse population and limited traffic where again large outlay on locomotive replacement is felt to be unjustified until the future of the railway itself can be more clearly defined.

The Austrian official attitude to railways, on the whole, however, though unsentimental, is not ambivalent. In governmental circles they are looked upon, for the most part, as a necessary service to which the public purse must be expected to contribute with as little question as it does to the maintenance of rivers and watercourses or the provision of the police or post-office. A cynic might note that the railwaymen's union is large and influential and that the successive post-war governments of Austria are likely to have considered very seriously the collective voting power of its members before taking decisions affecting or curtailing railways. Against this consideration, however, must be set the facts that only 20%

of the oil used in Austria is of home origin, that the hydro-electric power used for the generation of a major part of rail traction current is Austria's most plentiful indigenous source of energy and that rail routes can be kept open when roads are paralysed by severe winter weather. There is thus powerful logic in favour of a comprehensive railway system. Provision of private sidings, even in very recent developments, is on a scale not seen for at least a generation in Britain and the use of the narrow gauge for bulk through traffic is encouraged by the use both of conventional transporter trucks and also by the use of rollbocks, narrow gauge four wheeled trucks clamped under the standard gauge axles, a useful saving in dead weight. Nevertheless the narrow gauge is most under menace, both the Kuhnsdorf-Eisenkappel line and the Gurktalbahn, each in Carinthia, having been closed in the early seventies after comparatively trivial mishaps. Since the oil crisis of 1974 the threat appears to be less acute and one would like to think the relaxation is permanent. On a more prosaic plane it is probably true to say that nothing is retained in service – no item of equipment or rolling stock – for other than practical reasons nor discarded under the dictates of mere fashion. Thus although quite old items of rolling stock remain in use they do so because it is convenient to retain them and not as a conscious act of preservation.

This is not to say, however, that the railway authorities have taken a particularly mean or cavalier attitude to preservation. Stuffed steam locomotives both standard and narrow gauge, are preserved on display in the open at a number of places where they were to be seen during their working lives. 629.43 stands, for instance, outside the running shed at Linz and 91.32, formerly used on the branch to Neuberg, stands at the South end of the platform in Murzzuschlage.

At the railway museum in Vienna the following six locomotives are preserved inside the museum building.

Original owner	Name or class and number	Builder	Works No. and Date	BBÖ No.
KFNB	"AJAX" (No. 37)	Jones, Turner & Evans	23/1841	-
Südliche Staatsbahn	"STEINBRUCK"	Haswell	87/1848	-
kk priv. erste. Eisenbahngesellschaft	"GMUNDEN" (No. 4)	Wr. Neustadt	131/1854	-
Direction für den Staatsbahnbetrieb.	AR/254	Floridsdorf	445/1883	1.20 (sectioned)
Gaisbergbahn	1	Esslingen	2205/1886	
kk St. B	180.01	Floridsdorf	1343/1900	

and a further eight including 214.10 in the open

BB4O Class and number	Builder	Works No. and Date	ÖBB Class number
214.10	Floridsdorf	3101/1936	12.10
113.02	St. EG	4694/1923	33.102
81.44	Wr. Neustadt	5754/1923	58.744
270.125	Floridsdorf	2617/1920	156.3423
73.79	Wr. Neustadt	3169/1887	55.5708
60.115	Wr. Neustadt	4221/1899	54.14
10.13	Wr. Neustadt	4995/1910	15.13
310.23	St. EG	3791/1911	16.08

Vandalism is not an Austrian trait and locomotives kept in the open suffer, in general, only from the weather but clearly storage in the open is, ultimately, only slow destruction. In Vienna, at least, it is the hope ultimately to have all exhibits under cover but it doubtful if such intentions exist outside the capital.

During the tourist season the Zillertalbahn runs two daily return steam trains, the Steiermarkische Landesbahnen run a single steam working on Saturdays only on the Prëding to Stainz branch, a single return working between Birkfeld and Weiz each Wednesday, Thursday and Saturday from early July to early September and sundry steam specials on the Murtalbahn. On the standard gauge the private Montafonerbahn runs two trips each Thursday by steam from mid June to mid September using former ÖBB 0-8-0T No. 92.2231 (Krauss, Linz, 1909). Until 1979 a Gölsdorf 178 Class 0-8-0T had been used but was taken out of service because the cost of a replacement boiler was too high.

These workings attract a following large enough to make them worthwhile from a financial point of view but the attitude of most of the passengers is characterised by hilarity rather than reverence. It is as an unusual or, perhaps, nostalgic, background to conviviality that most are seen. Despite the goodwill towards steam which is thus kept alive the atmosphere of wine, bread and dripping and accordion music with which it tends to be associated has a somewhat off-putting effect on the rather more limited body of dedicated enthusiasts undertaking serious study of railways and their history or engaged in preservation in the way in which the latter has come to be understood in Great Britain. This may sound priggish but it is essentially true. The "bummel-zug" passengers are there because the steam train represents something old and, by inference, quaint. The preserver or historian would probably prefer to see the railway and the train left with its dignity rather more intact. It is a question of degree. Not all of the archaelogical group are priggish nor all the bummelzugers superficial and the two categories merge and blend at the edges. Private preservation effort does not yet exist on a scale comparable to that to be found in Great Britain but against that it must be remembered that the preservation movement reached its present scale in Britain from reaction against the closures that resulted from the Beeching plan. Austrian railways have not yet suffered this type of misfortune. There are no large mileages of closed branches or secondary main lines which it is desirable or attractive to save from destruction. It would have been admirable if there had been a concerted movement to preserve examples of the standard gauge classes which were scrapped in the sixties but it was only with the threat to narrow gauge steam in the late sixties and seventies that the four active preservation societies came into being.

These four principal private preservation efforts are the VKEF, Club 598, Club 760 and the ÖGEG. The former, the Verein der Karntner Eisenbahnfreunde (Carinthian Railway Enthusiasts Society) have been responsible for the operation of a length of 3.40km of the closed Gurktalbahn from Treibach-Althofen, the junction with the main line, to Pockstein-Zwischenwassern, together with the narrow gauge yard at Treibach. Former ÖBB locomotives preserved by the VKEF are:

298.102 – 0-6-2T	(former Steyrtalbahn), withdrawn 1973 (Kr. Li. 1994/1888)
498.08 – 0-6-2T	with superheat (formerly Class Uh) withdrawn 1973 (F1. 3038/1931)
898.01 – 0-6-0T	(ex. Kreis Kreuznachen Kleinbahnen via Heeresfeldbahn), withdrawn 1973 (Kr. Li. 1467/1926)
199.02 – 0-8-2T	former Class P) withdrawn 1973 (Kr. Li. 1467/1926)
499.01 – 0-10-0T	(former Class Kh) withdrawn 1973 (Kr. Li. 1262/1924)

but the society has also secured a number of coaches and wagons, an ex-Ybbs tramcar, eight industrial steam locomotives, various internal combustion locomotives and service vehicles, some of industrial origin, and two industrial electric locomotives.

Club 598 and Club 760 both have less ambitious objectives, which do not include track and buildings. The former preserves ÖBB locomotives 598.02 and 598.03 (both 0-6-4T by Krauss, Linz, works numbers 3357 and 8 of 1896) formerly used on the Ybbstalbahn until 1973 and kept at Waidhofen an der Ybbs where ÖBB also have the third member of the class (works No. 3356) on display. Club 760 working with the Steiermarkische Landesbahnen, has former ÖBB 398.01, a Krauss, (Linz) 0-6-4 (works number 5330, 1905) of the former NÖLB and 699.01, one of the ex Heeresfeldbahn 0-8-0T plus tender locomotives, together with the St. LB 0-6-2T Bh1 (Kr. Li. 5330/1905) and 0-6-0T No. 6 (Kr. Li. 2885/1893).

The degree of mutual trust and interdependence and the relaxed relationship that exists at Murau between Club 760 and its hosts, the Steiermarkische Landesbahnen, is evidence of an arrangement working well.

The ÖGEG (Österreichische Gesellschaft für Eisenbahngeschichte – Austrian Society for Railway History) at Linz was formed in 1974 with the aim of furthering the study of railway history and to preserve interesting locomotives, steam, diesel and electric, as well as rolling stock. With a membership of over 500 at the end of 1981 the ÖGEG possesses three standard gauge steam locomotives of the classes 78 (4-6-4T), 52 and 93 (2-8-2T), the former two with Giesl Ejector and Superheat Booster, several ex-ÖBB four and eight wheel coaches, and equipment for the electric tram at St. Florian near Linz, now operated by the Society.

A substantial number of Class 52 and 152 locomotives, withdrawn from traffic, still stood at their former depots in the Summer of 1980. Such were to be seen, for instance, at Bruck a.d. Mur, Vienna Nord, Linz and Sigmundsherberg. There is no official evidence that they constitute any kind of reserve but the fact that they were there, greased and with covers on the chimneys and that there has been no haste to cut them up inevitably brings to mind the thought that someone in the hierarchy may have had his eye on the oil situation.

Apart, however, from these whose future is, officially at least, destined to be the scrap yard, the following standard gauge locomotives are set aside for permanent retention, generally in moveable condition and mostly in, or near, working order.

Original owner	Class/ number	Builder	Works No. and date	Last owner	Where kept	Wheel Arrangement
Sudbahn	(29) 671	St. EG.	504-1860	GKB 671	GKB Graz	0-6-0
Sudbahn	(32d¹) 1851	Kr. Linz	3932/1898	GKB 1851	GKB Graz	0-6-0T
kk. St. B	169/02	Flor.	2091/1912	ÖBB 197.302	Knittelfeld	0-12-0RT
kk. St. B	169/03	Flor.	2092/1912	ÖBB 197.303	Knittelfeld	0-12-0RT
kk. St. B	69/01	Flor.	732/1890	ÖBB 97.201	Knittelfeld	0-6-2RT
kk.St. B	429/1971	St. EG.	4147/1916	ÖBB 35.233	Wien	2-6-2
Sudbahn	109/13	WN.	5080/1912	ÖBB 38.4101	Wien	4-6-0
ÖBB	42/2708	Flor.	17591/1946	ÖBB 42.2708	Wien	2-10-6
DR.	52/3503	Kr. Maff.	16629/1943	ÖBB 52.3503	Wien	2-10-0
DR.	52.7594	Flor.	16942/1944	ÖBB 52.7594	Wien	2-10-0
kk. St. B	80.988	WN.	5285/1915	ÖBB 57.223	Wien	0-1-0
Sudbahn	480.01	St. EG.	4358/1921	ÖBB 257.601	Wien	0-10-0
Sudbahn	580.03	St. EG.	3826/1912	ÖBB 258.902	Wien	2-10-0
BBÖ	12.02 (rebuilt from 0-6-0T kk. St. B No. 97.152 – 1898)	Flor.	3822/1935	ÖBB 69.002	Wien	2-2-2T
kk. St. B	29.22	BMMF	432/1912	ÖBB 175.817	Wien	2-6-2T
Sudbahn	629.01	St. EG.	3883/1913	ÖBB 77.66	Wien	4-6-2T
NÖLB	1.05	Kr. Linz	5396/1906	ÖBB 88.61	Wien	0-4-0T
BBÖ	378.121	Flor.	2981/1928	ÖBB 93.1421	Wien	2-8-2₁T
kk. St. B	69.08	Flor.	820/1892	ÖBB 97.208	Wien	0-6-2RT
kk. St. B	269.01	Flor.	2090/1912	ÖBB 197.301	Wien	0-12-0RT
BBÖ	DT1.07	Flor.	3081/1935	ÖBB 3071.07	Wien	2.4-2T
kk. St. B	220.222	WN	5444/1917	CSD 354.0130	Wien	2-6-2T
Sudbahn	(32C) 1663	St. EG.	2466/1895	MAV. 333.002	Wien	0-6-0

Original owner	Class/ number	Builder	Works No. and date	Last owner	Where kept	Wheel Arrangement
E.W.A.	21	Kr.Munich	1186/1882	Felten E Guillaume "ILSE"	Wien	0-4-0T
Sudbahn	(17c)372	Flor.	768/1891	GKB. 372	Wien	4-4-0
kk. St. B	30.27	Kr. Linz	4272/1900	OAM. 600.2	Wien	2-6-2T
BBÖ	478.10	WN.	5781/1927	ÖBB 392.2510	Wien	0-8-0T
Sulmtal-bahn 2	WN		4033/1897	ÖBB 394.02	Wien	2-6-2T
D.R.	52.844	Chrz.	1465/1941	ÖBB 52.844	Amstetten	2-10-0
BBÖ	378.26	Flor.	2929/1927	ÖBB 93.1326	Amstetten	2.8-2T
BBÖ	378.155	Flor.	3004/1931	ÖBB 93.1455	Amstetten	2.8-2T

It is from this pool of locomotives that the motive power is drawn for steam specials and commemorative trains.

Also at Amstetten (owned by ÖGEG) are a further Class 52 (No. 3316 by Jung. 11327 of 1944) and a Class 86. 2-8-2T (No. 476 by Deutsche Werk Kiel Aktiengesellschaft, 461 of 1943). At St. Pölten ÖBB depot there is a group of four locomotives owned by Herr Brenner of Elin-Union comprising:

2-10-0	52.7612	(Flor. 16960 – 1944)
2-6-0T	91.107	(Kr. Linz 6023 – 1908)
2-8-2T	93.1422	(Flor. 2982 – 1928)
0-6-2RT	97.203	(Flor. 734.1890)

These are all believed to be in working order.

All the locomotives listed above as in ÖBB depots, are scheduled as preserved except Sulmtalbahn No. 2 which is categorised merely as "stored". At the moment there is no shortage of steam fitters, drivers or firemen and reasonable availability of consumable stores and spare parts to carry out running shed repairs. What will happen when a locomotive requires general repair is less certain.

Historically the repair of locomotives in Austria was organised on a basis rather different to that prevailing in the United Kingdom. Just as it was commonplace here for a major railway to build its own locomotives but very rare for this to happen in Austria so in Austria it was much commoner than in Britain for major repairs or the making of major items of components for repairs to be placed with contractors. Nevertheless the kk St. B and its predecessors did own central repair works. Indeed the St. EG Locomotive Works (or Haswell's as it was known until he retired in 1885), though thought of as a major contracting works was, in fact, the works of the State Railway Company. "Patria" the first locomotive built in Austria, was constructed at the Floridsdorf repair shops of the KFNB where the master mechanic was an English ex-patriate named Baillie. In the latter part of the nineteenth century major rebuilds were undertaken there. The Nord West Bahn also had a repair works at Floridsdorf (Jedlersdorf) so that an otherwise obscure Viennese suburb had three locomotive works, the third being the celebrated Wiener Locomotivfabrik. The Sudbahn also had shops in Vienna as did the St. EG at Simmering. Provincial repair shops were at Gmund in Lower Austria, Linz in Upper Austria, Knittelfeld in Styria and Salzburg in

Salzburgland. The works of the GKB are in Graz and contained, at least until the end of steam in 1977, (and may contain them yet) the adjuncts of a traditional locomotive works, retaining the facilities for making and repairing rivetted boilers including a rivet heading machine for making rivets from round iron stock. It would be a source of delight if such treasures could be kept but, with the economic pressures of the present time, difficult to believe that their existence is secure.

Illustrations

BAVARIA   1851

SERAING   1851

WIENER NEUSTADT   1851

VINDOBONA   1851

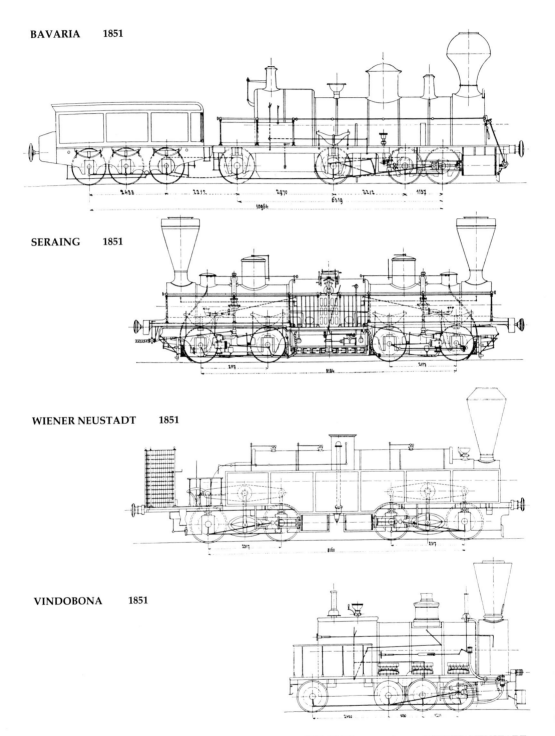

The Semmering protagonists, top BAVARIA, centre top SERAING, centre lower WIENER NEUSTADT, bottom VINDOBONA.

Southern State Railway Engerths No. 610 (top) and No. 628 (lower), both by John Cockerill of Seraing (Belgium) illustrate the changes in appearance, notably in boiler mountings, which occurred in the two year interval (from 1854 to 1856) between them. The decision to have these locomotives built in Belgium as opposed to ordering them from the newly formed and struggling native locomotive builders was one cause of the bitter personal differences between Engerth and John Haswell, the latter speaking not only for himself but for his Austrian competitors as well. They were rebuilt as 0-8-0 tender locomotives in the company's own shops in Vienna in 1861 and 1865 respectively, both then lasting until well into this century.

This picture of No. 622, a sister engine of No. 610, shows how the Engerths appeared after their rebuilding into 0-8-0 tender locomotives.

The American maid of all work translated to Central Europe. Norris of Philadelphia delivered their No. 339 to the state railway authorities in 1846. In some ways typically American in other details – for instance chimney, footplate, buffers and bufferbeams – it was very Austrian. The locomotive was unbraked but the tender had wooden brake blocks actuated by the vertical spindle and handle which can be seen.

No. 818 of the Südbahn was one of the class of 4-4-0's known on the Südbahn as the 15A's, built at the shops of Wenzel Gunther (No. 78/1848) from 1848 to 1850. This is a sister engine to the STEINBRUCK (No. 827), now preserved in the Vienna Railway Museum.

No. 649 of the Südbahn was built for the Southern State Railway in 1856 by Gunther in Wiener Neustadt. In 1867 the Südbahn gave up the struggle to keep it running in its original form and rebuilt it as a 0-8-0 tender locomotive.

Südbahn No. 152 was built in 1856 by Sigl for the Tiroler Staatsbahn which was amalgamated into the Südbahn before its official opening.

The opening of the Arlbergbahn in 1884 was an epoch making event not only in the magnitude of the undertaking itself but also in marking the re-entry of the state into railway ownership and the inauguration of a new era in locomotive design. No. 28.01 built by Krauss, Munich for the opening of the line used, for the first time in an Austrian passenger locomotive, the 2-6-0 arrangements, Heusinger (Walschaert) valve gear, and a Helmholtz leading truck. Originally the A1V class they were later Class 9 and finally Class 28.

It is interesting to compare the similarities of detail – chimney, dome, sandbox, safety valves, – of the 0-8-0T supplied by Krauss for goods work on the Arlberg with the passenger locomotive from the same maker. This is Krauss No. 1500/1884 (No. 505 of the kk St. B). Originally Class VII, as here, they were finally Class 78.

An early picture of the Westbahnhof in Vienna, the overall roof of which is flanked by twin towers. The train in Platform 1 is one of the original 2-4-0's of the KEB (later Class 12 of the kk St. B) put into service in 1858. The vehicle on the siding on the right of the picture is a luggage van with lavatory.

Zell/Griebl

The original 2-4-0's of the KEB, built between 1858 and 1863 (to a total of 54) had lives of forty to forty-five years during which, not unexpectedly they were much rebuilt. The picture below shows kk St. B No. 12.20 (formerly No. 34 ULMERFELD of the KEB) as rebuilt during the regime of Littrow in the early days of the kk St. B, with standard cab, replacement boiler, and the type of spark arrestor disrespectfully referred to as the "dovecote" or, worse still, the "Pigeon coop". The upper picture shows KEB No. 11 (TRAUN) one of the original batch of 1858 (Wiener Sigl Works No. 238) in an intermediate stage with a non-standard cab but one, nevertheless, which was a great improvement upon the original open footplate.

Slezak

One of the later 2-4-0's supplied by St. EG to the KEB in 1880 was No. 30 HAAG later kk St. B 7.05 (Works No. 1555) which, rebuilt as shown and fitted with the automatic vacuum brake, remained in use until 1917.

A photograph dating from 1908 of KEB No. 207 (St. EG 1557/1880) running as kk St. B No. 708, seen here outside Vienna Westbahnhof It remained at Vienna West shed until the mid-twenties.

Ost. Eisenbahnmuseum

If the KEB 2-4-0's had long lives those of the standard 0-6-0 goods classes were even longer. KEB No. 169 (Sigl 1062/1871) (below) was already sixty-seven years old when it was taken over by the DRB after the Anschluss in 1938. The earlier picture (above) shows No. 102 (Sigl. 622/1868) in new condition at the maker's works, with the original design of spark arrestor. Examples of the class outlived the second war. The ingredients of their success were reliability and gentleness with lightly laid or sharply curved track, combined with a surprisingly sprightly performance.

Slezak

Slezak

Tank locomotives were not common in Austria when the KEB took delivery from Hartmann of five 0-6-0T (Works Nos. 657 to 661 inclusive in 1873). In the picture No. 61.04 (KEB No. 178 – Works No. 660) stands before the round-house in Salzburg, apart from the 1902 type replacement boiler, not much altered from its original form. She ran until the late twenties.

Slezak

The classic Hall type 0-6-0 (Sigl No. 674/1868) one of 56 such machines used by the KFJB. The example shown was their No. 63 later kk St. B 35.13 fitted with replacement boiler and cab and equipped with automatic vacuum brakes. One of the duties of the class was the working of the Donauuferbahn, a line along the banks of the Danube in Vienna linking the numerous wharves and factories but also carrying passengers and this photo was taken in Brigittenau Station on that line.

The KFNB Class IId (later Class 308 of the kk St. B) was built between 1895 and 1907 when interest in the Atlantic type was at its highest. They were high steppers suited to the longer runs and relatively level terrain of their native railway but in BBÖ days tended to find themselves outclassed for the main expresses whilst not sufficiently versatile for lesser duties. The last two just survived into DRB ownership in 1938.

Like the KEB (most by East/West) which it both joined and crossed the KPRB, a predominantly North/South railway, had a large part of its mileage in mountain terrain and had a high proportion of 0-6-0 locomotives. This very early picture, dating from 1869, shews one of them in Huttenberg, the Northern terminal of the then newly opened branch from Launsdorf (on the main line from Villach to St. Michael and the North), built to serve the mines at Huttenberg, (in the right back ground).

In 1882 the KPRB turned from 2-4-0 to 4-4-0 tender locomotives for its expresses. This is their No. 268 (Wiener Neustadt 2867/1884), of the second series, at Landeck as originally delivered.

The Niederosterreichische Sudwestbahn was another railway – a minor one this time – which relied upon 0-6-0 locomotives for its motive power. This picture, taken in the opening year, 1877, at the Southern terminus of the long branch south from Pöchlarn at the KEB main line shows the station-house which still stands. Later Kienburg Gaming was linked to Waidhofen by the 760mm Ybbstalbahn over the watershed and down the Ybbs valley.

For lighter duties the NOSWB used seven 0-4-0T locomotives. The top picture (right) shows No. 6C, Wiener Neustadt 2487/1881 later kk St. B 8506, rebuilt with a self-firing arrangement in 1905. The lower picture shows its sister engine No. 8504 (No.2463/1881) in original condition.

Slezak

No. 2 AIGEN of the Mühlkreisbahn (Krauss Linz No. 1901/1887). A 0-6-0T with well tanks, it was later 494.62 of the kk St. B and BBÖ by the latter of whom it was sold in the early 1930's into industrial use. It is preserved outside the sugar factory at Hohenau, in Lower Austria.

The celebrated RITTINGER (Wiener Neustadt 1657/1873) exhibited at the 1873 Vienna Exhibition and bought in 1874 by the ONWB. The photograph illustrates the classic Hall arrangement of external cranks and valve gear. The engine ran as ONWB No. 81, and after 1909 as kk St. B. 201.01.

Zell/Griebl

RITTINGER in old age. In this picture the old war-house, with rebuilt cab, and altered valve gear and fitted with the vacuum brake is seen employed, in the latter days, on more tamely domestic duties than the Vienna Prague expresses with which it earned its fame.

The general run of 4-4-0's on the ONWB up to the time of the RITTINGER had been of the widely used long-boiler type. Those of the type in the picture were built between 1870 and 1873, designated Classes IIIa and IIIb on the ONWB and latter Class 16 on the kk St. B by whom they were equipped with better cabs and the vacuum brake.

The ONWB marked the new century by changing its long established adherance to the 0-6-0 and 0-8-0 type for goods work by introducing the Class XVIIb 2-6-0 two cylinder saturated steam compounds. No. 265 is shown here sporting its kk St. B number (360.15) after the ONWB had been taken over by the state in 1908.

Floridsdorf official photo

No. 403 was one of the combined locomotives and luggage vans designed by Elbel for ONWB branches and built at Floridsdorf (No. 291/1880). They lasted until the first world war.

Slezak

Apart from early examples in the 1830's and 40's British locomotives were rare in Austria. In 1884, however, the St. EG ordered a Webb-type compound 2-4-0 (or 2-2-2-0) from Sharp Stewart of Manchester (Works No. 3163) mainly for experimental purposes. It was largely unsuccessful and spent most of its short life in store but in 1896 it was brought and used as a mobile test bed by Gölsdorf then about to embark upon his compound designs.

Slezak

The French influence very apparent, a 2-4-2 of St. EG Class I in original condition double heads a train with a rebuilt example of the same class in kk St. B days. The leading engine is kk St. B 5.10 (Hanomag 1592/1883). Note the Westinghouse pump and also the speed indicator on the bracket suspended from the running plate by the second coupled axle.

Ost. Eisenbahnmuseum

The eighteen 0-6-0 locomotives of St. EG Class IVf[n] (later kk St. B Class 231) were built between 1890 and 1897 and stationed at Vienna East where they were used for goods, slow passenger and shunting work.

Upper picture. F. Strauss from the collection of F. Krauss

2-4-0's of Class 18 (in the 1864 classification) of the Südbahn were in production from 1859 until 1872. In the upper picture No. 475, one of the last (Wiener Neustadt 1517/1872) to be built is shown in original condition hauling a passenger train on the Vienna link railway near Modling in 1894. At high level in the background is the Vienna South running shed.

Lower picture. Ost. Nationalbibliothek

Collection H. G. Keller

Early in this century, in this photo by Hirzel, Südbahn No. 399 (Floridsdorf 1010/1896) is shown standing in the station at Kufstein (Tyrol) with a fast train for Innsbruck. Note the vacuum brake equipment on the cab roof.

Zell/Griebl

Ever increasing train weights led the Sudbahn on from 4-4-0's to 4-4-2's. Here No. 221 (St. EG 3470/1908) is passing through Vienna-Atzgersdorf with a 300 tonne train for Semmering, a duty said to have been particularly in Louis Göldsorf's mind when they were put in hand.

Slezak

The four examples of Südbahn Class 9 were built by St. EG in 1900. The engine in the picture is No. 1403 (Works No. 2896), later No. 9.403 of the BBÖ in whose hands it ran until 1938.

Slezak

Just as the 4-6-0 epitomised express locomotive design in the immediate pre-war years so the 4-6-2T which was its tank equivalent came into high favour. Prossy's Class 629 on the Südbahn, of which this is No. 629.05 (St. EG 3887/1913), was powerful, versatile and kind to the track as well as appealing to the eye. It was soon adopted as a kk St. B standard design and continued to be built in Czechoslovakia until the middle of the second war.

Until the opening of the Arlberg tunnel in 1884 the Vorarlbergerbahn led a chaste existence detached from the other railways of Austria its trains hauled by two locomotive classes, 2-4-0 for passenger work and 0-6-0 for goods, supplied by Krauss of Munich. In the top picture is No. 6 HOHENEMS (Krauss 163/1872) and in the lower, No. 18 VADUZ (Krauss 145/1872). There were six 2-4-0's and four 0-6-0's originally, supplemented by a further three 0-6-0's from St. EG in 1876 and these latter survived into BBO days, the last being withdrawn in 1927.

When the kk St. B Class 6 compound 4-4-0's came out in 1894 they handled some of the very best trains on the state system. In this picture taken at Amstetten in 1895 No. 603 (Floridsdorf 917/1894) is heading the westbound Orient Express which it would take through to Salzburg. Early examples were allocated to Vienna West but after the 206 Class came out in 1903 the 6's were largely dispersed to provincial depots. Twenty went to BBÖ the remaining 48 being divided between Czechoslovakia and Poland.

The quest for the ideal spark arrestor meant that design was seldom static and it is ironic that it was not until steam was in its last days that the combination of Dr Giesl-Gieslingen's Giesl ejector with his micro-spark arrestor came near to a total solution of the spark problem. The arrestor being carried by kk St. B No. 106-80 is a revised type for which Johann Rihosek (Gölsdorf's right hand man) was responsible in 1906. This example had a short life as in 1909 the locomotive was transferred to Galicia and converted to oil firing.

Pawlik Collection

Not even the greatest admirer of the Class 9 4-6-0's of the kk St. B could have described the appearance of them as handsome though they were doughty performers. Outside frames had been an enduring feature of Austrian locomotive design, though by no means universal, but Gölsdorf had already abandoned them as part of his settled policy and used them on the Class 9's solely because in this instance he needed the extra space between the frames. Not long after this he paid the visit to England which stirred his interest in the clean external lines which characterised his later locomotives.

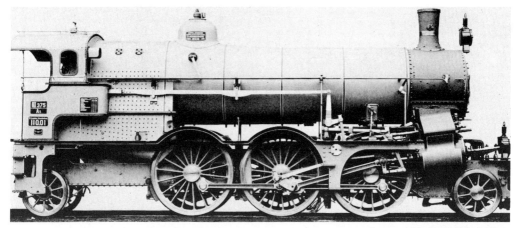

Floridsdorf Works photo

One of the most talked of designs of this century was Gölsdorf's 2-6-2 Class 110 in which by lateral thinking he succeeded in marrying the features that had given the long-boiler type its consistent appeal in Austria (namely easy passage on sharp curves and unfettered firebox dimensions) into a thoroughly modern express locomotive by the use of a Helmholtz leading truck and a trailing truck placed behind the fire box. The good riding, clean lines and sinuous movement of the 110's gave them an appeal which never deserted them. This is the first (Floridsdorf No. 1505), completed and tested in December 2904 and delivered to the kk St. B in January 1905.

Lemmel was one of the most noted of pre-1914 Austrian railway photographers (at a time when the authorities did their best to discourage photography!). Here, about 1910, he has caught 210.01 in which the 2-6-2 arrangement was developed (in 1908) into the 2-6-4. The class were used for the Vienna-Cracow expresses for which Rayl and Simon had designed the KFNB Pacifics (never built) but only one out of the eleven in the class was shedded in Vienna and after 1918 they were allocated to Poland.

2-6-2T No. 229.115 (Floridsdorf 1988/1911 about to depart from Graz main station with a train for the secondary main line eastwards to Gleisdorf and Fehring *c*. 1913.

113

A view down the erecting shop, *c.* 1900, of the St. EG works in Vienna showing five locomotives of Class 30 (2-6-2T) in progress in the foreground and a Sudbahn 4-4-0 (Class 106) in the background. The shop was modern and equipped with an 80 tonne electric overhead crane, the factory was prosperous and full of work and its name and products were internationally known yet scarcely thirty-five years later both the firm and the works had vanished and other buildings stood on the site.

Handy and reliable 0-6-0 tender engines appealed to the military authorities on both sides in both world wars, as witness, for instance, the Dean goods to the British Army. In this 1914/18 picture a military driver poses beside 56.110 (Wiener Neustadt 3634/1892).

The solitary example of Class 100.01, equipped with oil-firing in an attempt to mitigate the smoke problem in the tunnels of the Tauern route, standing in Bischofshofen on 8th August, 1913 under preparation for a working to the South.

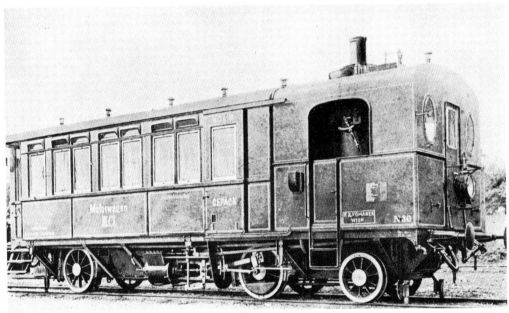

The NÖLB, plagued by lightly trafficked lines which, for political and social reasons, it had to operate made the most persistent attempt to employ steam railcars on both standard and 760mm lines. This is No. 30, the first of the second batch of standard gauge cars delivered in 1905/6 by Komarek of Vienna and used between Korneuberg (the junction with the main line) and Ernstbrunn. All had been sold by 1920.

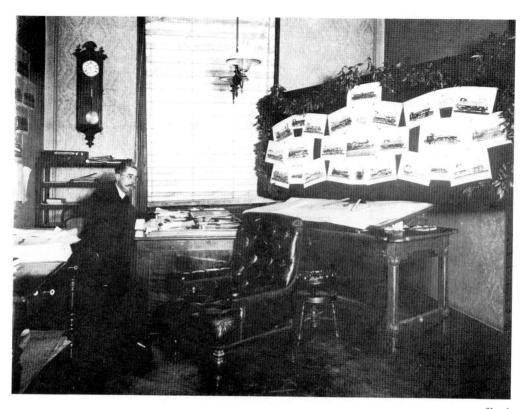

The master in his office. Karl Gölsdorf posed for this picture on 24th February, 1906. The montage facing him (right of the picture) depicts 26 locomotive classes designed under his direction.

Between 1895 and 1900 the EWA had five 4-4-0's (of the same design as the kk St. B Class 4) from Wiener Neustadt of which this is the first, EWA No. 31, Works No. 3799. This and its sister engine No. 32 survived to become DRB No. 367002 respectively in 1938 but the other three were withdrawn in 1936.

The Schneebergbahn opened in 1897 and was worked by the EWA from 1899. With it the EWA took over, inter alia, a class of three 0-4-0T by Wiener Neustadt of which this is No. 2 (Works No. 3908, 1896), later EWA No. 26 and later still, after the 1938 Anschluss, DRB 88 7202.

F. Rizicka Collection

2-4-0 No. 25 of the KFJB, built by Sigl in Vienna (Works No. 1045/1870), seen here as kk St. B 24.25.

Johann Brotan, a Czech citizen of the Austrian Empire, was a senior engineer of the kk St. B under Gölsdorf. In the closing years of the last century he perfected the design of his patent locomotive boiler in which, broadly speaking, the steam and water spaces were separated into separate barrels and the firebox was formed of a close set row of large diameter water tubes, insulated on the outside with fireclay and enclosed in a steel casing. This is the first such boiler to be placed in service on the kk St. B, early in 1901, in an old 0-6-0 (No. 47.54) inherited from the KEB. This transplant was done at Pilsen where this photo (by Hobek of Pilsen) was taken though the locomotive was afterwards stationed at Triest. The kk St. B later built some of the Class 174 0-8-0's with similar boilers but few Brotan boilers were used in German Austria though relatively widely on the MAV and on other systems to the East and South East. Its objective was the more efficient combustion of coals of low calorific value and/or poor physical characteristics in which it had some success but at the expense of much increased complexity.

118

The Kremstalbahn ran southwards from Linz to Bad Hall, financed, in a considerable degree, by Krauss money. In these circumstances it is no great surprise to find that its ten locomotives came from the Krauss works at Linz. It became part of the kk St. B in 1902. Above is 89.02 (Works No. 3122/1894) and below 83.37 (Works No. 1688/1887) in their state railway days. The 2-4-0 design was produced by Krauss for use in Bavaria. In the lower picture, taken in Bad Hall, the train staff have been joined by the station staff and the local postman.

both Ost. Eisenbahnmuseum

The KFNB, linking two of the leading cities (Vienna and Cracow) of the old Empire and having a well laid and relatively level road, had besides links in its origins and early personnel with English railway practice. All these are reflected in the two locomotives shewn on this page, the 2-4-0 MAZEPPA, built by St. EG (under John Haswell) of 1857 and the 2-2-2 RAKETE by Sigl, Vienna (Works No. 50/1862).

The KFNB continued to build single-driver express locomotives. FULTON (above) was built by the firm of Strousberg of Linden near Hanover (Works No. 543) in 1871. The final fling of the 2-2-2 on the KFNB was a class of four delivered by Floridsdorf in 1873. These were rebuilt in 1883 into 2-4-0's in the form shown below, in which they lasted until *c.* 1912. The RAKETE (on the previous page) and its four sisters were rebuilt in the same way but the FULTON and the three other Strousberg locomotives of the same class were not deemed worth rebuilding and were scrapped.

In its early days the KFNB used small wheeled 2-2-0's for its freight and mixed traffic but from 1863 onwards began to make increasing use of the 0-6-0. Here a Sigl -built 0-6-0 is shown in kk St. B days bearing the number 43.02.

By strange coincidence the KFNB Class VIII 2-6-0's later became Class 260 of the kk St. B. Built by Wiener Neustadt the class represented both a decisive move towards larger locomotives – the standard goods engine for over thirty years had been the 0-6-0 – and a vote of confidence in the use of compounding into which both Rayl (of the KFNB) and Gölsdorf of the kk St. B had been conducting experiments. No. 553 shewn dated from 1896 and was later kk St. B 260.33.

By 1913 the former KFNB Atlantics dating from 1895 (kk St. B Class 308) were becoming pressed to capacity by the operating department and three of them were rebuilt as 4-6-0's (as shewn above) with the driving wheel diameter reduced from 2000 to 1614mm, giving a corresponding reduction of maximum speed from 100 to 80kph, being then retitled Class 227. No more were so treated and it may be inferred that the level of improvement did not justify the expense.

Like its neighbour the Kaiserin Elizabeth Bahn the KRB relied heavily on 0-6-0 locomotives. The MARIA SAAL above, with outside frames but inside valve gear was built by Sigl in Wiener Neustadt, one of the earliest locomotives to be delivered after the move from Vienna (Works No. 672/1869).

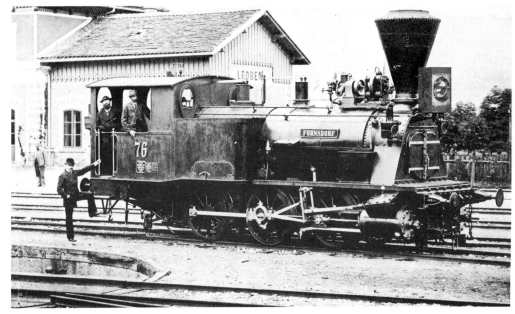

Zell Griebl

KRB No. 76 (Krauss, Munich No. 193/1872) was one of the first locomotives to be provided with an electric head light, supplied by a Sedlaczek dynamo and small reciprocating steam engine on the boiler top. The engine (later kk St. B 62.01) worked on the mineral branch from Zellweg to Fohnsdorf.

Ost. Eisenbahnmuseum

The KRB was one of the few Austrian railways to make use of locomotives built by the Swiss Locomotive Works at Winterthur. This 0-6-0T is KRB No. 112 (1874) which originally carried the name MANGART but which is shewn here as kk St. B No. 63.02., fitted with a replacement boiler. The three locomotives of the class spent many years on shunting duties at Knittelfeld and the last was in service until 1929.

When the KRB took over the working of the Zeltweg to Fohnsdorf mineral branch from the mine owners, the Vordernberger Erzverein (forerunners of the State Mining Corporation, Alpine Montangesellschaft) they inherited this curious one-off by the firm of F. Wöhlert, Berlin, (Works No. 316/1871). It was taken over by the kk St. B with its parent railway and lasted until 1902.

The 0-8-0's of the St. EG Class Vg (1894) were noted for their enormous grate area (3.25m^2) in proportion to the total heating surface (188m^2), to accommodate which the rear pair of wheels were placed very far back. Belpaire fireboxes were not much used on Austrian locomotives other than on the St. EG. The class became kk St. B Class 175 but passed to Czechoslovakia in 1918, where the last was not withdrawn until 1968.

New foreign built locomotives were rare in Austria after 1880 because of the introduction of tariffs but the 0-4-0 tank (above) used on the Lokalbahn from Schwechat (near Vienna) to Mannersdorf was an exception being delivered by Hagans of Erfurt, Germany in 1884 (Works No. 156). It became 20001 of the St. EG and finally 283.01 of the kk St. B who disposed of it in 1911.

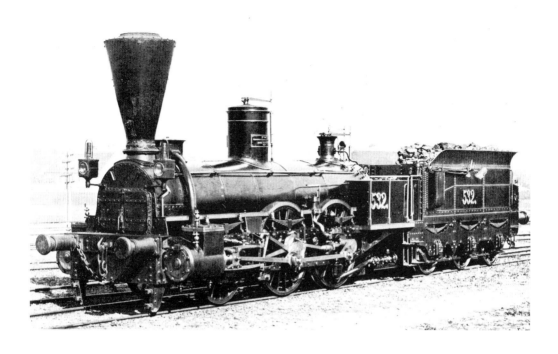

When the Südbahn company came into being in 1858 it inherited a number of very sound locomotive classes from its predecessors. Their Class 18 2-4-0's, illustrated by No. 532 (top picture) were designed for the Kaiser Ferdinands Orient Bahn but were actually delivered in 1858. No. 532 was built by Kessler of Esslingen and carried the works No. 461. The logical development of the class, soon put into effect, was into a 4-4-0 and No. 556 (bottom) delivered by Kessler in 1861 (Works No. 515) was one of Class 19 which was the result. Nineteen of the 2-4-0's came into the BBÖ stud in 1924 and the last ran in 1932. The whole 29 of the 4-4-0's survived to become BBÖ property in 1924 but were all withdrawn within five years. The BBÖ Classes were 118 for the 2-4-0's and 116 for the 4-4-0's.

both – Slezak

The Südbahn with two major trans-Alpine routes (the Brenner and the Semmering) and much other mountain route-mileage made extended use of the 0-8-0, with sideplay on the central coupled axles on Haswell's principle. No. 930 (Class 34) above was actually built at St. EG under Haswell's direction in 1867 (Works No. 787) as one of a class of ten built for and used exclusively on the Brenner line. Nine (including No. 930, in the picture) went to Italy when the line was divided and one to the BBÖ but was withdrawn before it was reclassified.

Südbahn No. 142 (St. EG No. 1223/1872), originally No. 13 of the GKB, represented an important shift in the direction of Austrian design. Hitherto the mounting of the boiler low and between the frames had been almost a fetish. In No. 142 inside frames and a high pitched boiler were paired in a manner later accepted as standard practice.

128

The 1873 Exhibition engine RITTINGER, though bought by the ONWB inspired the Südbahn to build their Class 17a 4-4-0's, followed by the 17 b's, such as Number 320 (above), built by Floridsdorf in 1884, (No. 492). Doubtless Karl Gölsdorf had plenty of opportunity of observing the good work done by these locomotives under his father's control for when he took charge of the kk St. B locomotive designs he proceeded to build his 4-4-0's of Classes 1 to 4 which carried on the same theme.

Südbahn No. 61 was one of the class of 14 combined locomotives and luggage vans put into service on the railway between 1879 and 1881, all from Floridsdorf.

Slezak

4-4-2 No. 108.33 of the kk St. B, one of the later examples of the class, built by First Bohemian, and shewn here in a works photograph when new in 1904. For a number of years this class handled the expresses on the former Franz Josef Bahn (Vienna to Prague) and all 25 examples owned by the kk St. B went to Czechoslovakia in 1918. The class, however, had also been adopted by Gölsdorf senior on the Sudbahn and eleven of them came to the BBÖ on the amalgamation in 1924, though like many Atlantic classes they were found to be outclassed by traffic requirements on the most important trains yet overpowered for secondary work so that they all went by about early 1933. The Czechs followed suit and all theirs were withdrawn by the end of 1937.

Slezak

The kk St. B Class 29 2-6-2T's were the superheated version of Class 229 and numbered only 36 engines but they were scattered over four divisions, Prague, Villach, Cracow and Vienna. By one of the curiosities of the 1918 division of the rolling stock twenty six of these came to the BBÖ and the last were in service until 1961.

No. 210.02, first of Gölsdorfs Class 2-6-4's, stands in the sunlight of a winter day at the outward end of Vienna Nordbahnhof at the start of a trial run. Gölsdorf is second from the left in the group.

Ost. Eisenbahnmuseum

329.78 (First Bohemian No. 323/1909) was fitted new with oil firing on Holden's system which required a small fire bed of coal (hence the coal on the tender) and was destined for service in Lemburg (now in Poland). Later it worked from Iglau but this notwithstanding it was one of those allocated to Austria in 1918.

Ost Eisenbahnmuseum

There was a considerable stud of Class 30 2-6-2T's stationed at Hütteldorf (West Vienna) for working the Stadtbahn (the Viennese equivalent of the Inner Circle), fitted with oil firing and condensing apparatus but No. 30.104 above, though based on Hütteldorf was not so fitted and was used on suburban duties.

In 1902 some of the shed staff at St. Michael posed with 0-6-0 No. 15944 (later 59.144) of the kk St. B.

Gölsdorf produced his compound 2-8-0's originally to handle expresses over the Arlberg section and, indeed, they introduced a new epoch on that line from their appearance in 1897, but they soon became accepted as heavy goods engines all over the system and 187 were built.

As a result of the building of the three experimental designs (later Classes 76, 78 and 79) the kk St. B arrived at the design of the Class 73 0-8-0 which eventually totalled 455 and was to be found, almost literally, everywhere on the system. No. 73.372 (top picture) was one of the last, delivered by St. EG in 1906. The BBÖ's share in 1918 was 10% i.e. 44 engines. These survived intact until the war but by 1951 were down to 36 and to one example by 1960, now preserved at the Austrian Railway Museum in Vienna.

When Class 73 was a quarter of a century old Gölsdorf decided that it was time that a more modern 0-8-0 was introduced but the 73's were so well liked for their capabilities and ease of maintenance that he produced a compromise in the Class 174 (of which 44 were made, including ten with Brotan boilers) in which he used the frames and enginework of a 73 with a more modern, high pitch boiler and up to date fittings.

Slezak

The last act in the evolution of the 19th century Austrian goods locomotive was the introduction of the ten coupler with the Class 180 (1900), designed originally for the heavy coal traffic of Bohemia and Moravia but soon used far more widely. BBÖ got 61 of them and a handful survived to receive DRB numbers. This is 180.535.

Gebruder Hardy photo – Ost. Eisenbahnmuseum

As train weights over the Arlberg route continued to increase they outstripped the capacity of the 2-8-0's of Class 170. By an almost inevitable progression Gölsdorf turned to a two cylinder compound 2-10-0, Class 280 in 1906. Three were built (Nos. 280.01, 280.02 and 280.03) and stationed at Landeck where they remained until electrification of the line. The last was broken up in 1931 when only 25 years old.

Photo by Lemml – Hermann Collection

The 2-6-0T's (Class 99) were in production from 1895 – 1907 and, in an amended version (the 199's), until 1914. The latter had single domes but many of the originals were reboilered with single dome boilers so that it is not an infallible test of identity.

Zell/Griebl

No. 409.27 (built 1901) after rebuilding by BBÖ as a simple expansion engine with poppet valves in 1924.

A scene at Hieflau in August, 1958 showing a Class 209 BBÖ No. 209.16 by then 38.4104 of the ÖBB with Giesl ejector. The locomotive was withdrawn the following year. Twenty three years later the scene is unchanged save for the disappearance of the steam locomotive.

Gölsdorf 2-6-4 No. 310.20 (1911) at Vienna Westbahnhof in 1936.

Zell/Griebl

When Lehner was asked to build a pair of fast small tank engines to haul light expresses he took two old 0-6-0T's of Class 97, first built in 1898 and rebuilt them as 2-2-2T's which he called Class 12. This photograph dates from 1939, after they had been renumbered by the DRB, but could easily have been taken in 1981 as the locomotive is stored in Vienna in working order.

Zell/Griebl

No. 214.13 the last of the batch of the class completed in 1936. The hood over the smoke box door was fitted as one of a series of experiments in smoke dispersal.

G. Gilnreiner

No. 214.11 (by that time renumbered 12.11 by the ÖBB) emerging from Weinzettel tunnel on its way over the Semmering with train No. D 983 on 20th June 1956.

Zell-Griebl

No. 30.80 standing at Rekawinkel (at the high point of the Vienna end of the western main line) with a local in 1936.

Zell Griebl

The former ONWB Class XVIIb became Class 360 of the BBÖ. Here No. 360.12 (dating from 1901) is seen standing outside the Nord Westbahnhof in Vienna in 1937. The class was by then being withdrawn slowly but the last survived until 1957.

Zell-Griebl

Three generations of rack-locomotives on the Erzbergbahn in 1950 outside the round-house at Vordernberg. They are (left to right) 2-12-2T No. 97.402 (built 1942), 0-12-0T No. 97.303 (formerly BBÖ 269.03) built 1912 and 0-6-2T No. 97.207 (formerly BBÖ 69.07) built 1892.

Slezak

The other 2-12-2T (No. 297.401) of the Erzbergbahn at Prabischl on 16th June, 1961. These were the most powerful rack locomotives in service anywhere in the world but loading limitations on the rack prevented their being used to their maximum capacity.

Zell-Griebl

Stored locomotives in the (by then) disused Nordwestbahnhof in Vienna in 1937. The slump had depressed requirements and the hope of their being used again seemed remote but traffic revived after the Anschluss (and the start of the war) and many (such as the 170 class 2-8-0 third from left) went back into service. The last Class 170 (by then ÖBB Class 56) ran until 1956.

E. Schmidt

A symbol of the changes in Austrian fortune, a 0-8-0 of BBÖ Class 73 (No. 154) in the Soviet zone in 1953, bearing Russian marking and a German running number.

J. Slezak

The Austrian equivalent of the Great Western pannier tank – Gölsdorf's 0-8-0T tank design of 1898 (BBÖ 178.802, ÖBB 92.2220) for branch line and siding work, in service at Hieflau in 1961.

Zell-Griebl

The standard 0-8-0T shunting class of the BBÖ with Lentz poppet valves. This is 478.12 standing at Vienna West in 1936.

Zell/Griebl

Gölsdorf's 199's (2-6-0T) were designed in 1908 for branches with severe axle loading restrictions and curvature and were one of the last of his classes to remain in use. This photo was taken at Vienna Franz Josef Bahnhof in 1937.

The first two post-war locomotives emerging from Floridsdorf Works in the Autumn of 1945. The two Kriegsloks 42.2701 (leading) and 42.2702 were almost a symbol of the Austrians' determination to lift themselves out of the misery in which they found themselves – militarily defeated, occupied and almost starving – but useful though the Class 42's were they were outlived by the Class 52's which, because of their lighter axle loadings, were more versatile.

ÖBB 71.516 (formerly BBÖ DT 1:16) in 1952 with a local train of four four-wheelers at Nussdorf, one of the wine villages on the northern outskirts of Vienna on the former Franz Josef Bahn.

Zell/Griebl

The large steam railcar built by Floridsdorf for the EWA in 1935 standing, when new, at the Aspangbahnhof in Vienna. Later it became BBÖ Number DT 2.01. It outlasted the war but the reliability and durability of the VT44 diesel railcars ruled out the possibility of its being repeated.

F. Meilinger

4-6-2T No. 629.77 an example of the class as developed on the BBÖ, with enlarged tanks and poppet valves, at Bruck an der Mur in 1931.

760mm gauge 0-4-0T No. 698.01 (Henschel 25701/1941) in St. Pölten Alpenbahnhof 1953. It was scrapped in 1969.

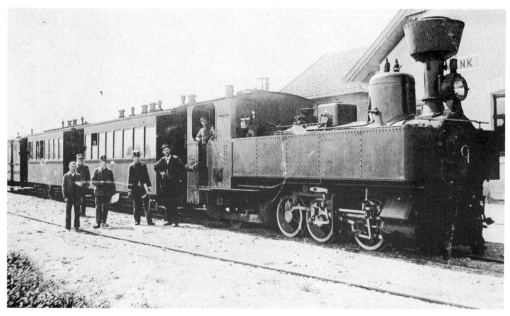

NÖLB No. 8, a 760mm gauge 0-6-02T by Krauss, Linz (Works No. 3870, 1898) in Mank Station about 1900.

C. Bellingradt. Collection of A. Luft

Superheated 0-6-2T No. Uh 05 (Krauss Linz 1512/1929) with its DRB number 99.825. The 'S' on the tank side indicates that flange lubricators were fitted.

Ost. Eisenbahnmuseum

Komarek four axle direct drive steam railcar No. 41 of the NÖLB 760mm Waldviertalbahn.

A. Luft

A scene in August 1957 in Weitra Station on the former Waldviertalbahn. The 0-8-0 tank plus tender locomotive is ÖBB 699.02 (formerly German Army 2822) built by Franco-Belge in 1944.

J. Slezak

760mm 0-6-2T ÖBB 398.01 (Krauss Linz 5330/1905) in Pfaffenschlag station near the summit of the Ybbstalbahn in 1959. The locomotive was withdrawn in 1973 and was purchased for preservation by Club 760.

A. Luft

Alpine narrow gauge exemplified. St.LB No. 6 (Krauss Linz 2885/1893) traverses the street at Hansenhütte on the Kapfenberg to Au line in July 1959.

A. Luft

760mm gauge 0-4-0T of th St. LB in Stainz Station, on the Preding-Stainz section with a train of standard gauge wagons on rollbocks, September, 1959. In 1969 the locomotive (Krauss Linz 2774/1892) was rebuilt with superheat and one man control and transferred to the Murtalbahn where it still runs.

A. Luft

760mm gauge 0-6-2T (St. LB No. U9, Krauss Linz 3063/1894), bought from BBÖ in 1922, being turned at Mauterndorf in February, 1958.

Preservation in action. ANNY of the preserved section of the Gurktalbahn in July 1975 curving away from the main line (at high level in right distance). The lcomotive, formerly in service with Böhler at Kapfenburg, (Krauss – Munich 7257 dates from 1916.

The 0-10-0T ÖBB 499.01 now preserved on the Gurktalbahn at work in Kuhnsdorf in the early spring of 1961. It is Krauss Linz No. 1262 of 1924.

Ost. Eisenbahnmuseum

One of the convertible 2-4-0T locomotives built in 1895 for the then 1106mm gauge Lambach-Gmunden line and regauged to standard in 1903.

Amidst the rolling beauty and tranquility of the Salzkammergut SKLB No. 10 (Krauss Linz 2822/1893) passes Enzersberg in July 1957.

SKLB No. 12 (Krauss Linz 5513/1906) near Lueg on the shores of the Wolfgangsee, July, 1957.

J. Stogermayr

The ultimate development of the Austrian 760mm 0-6-2T, and almost the swansong of the Krauss Linz Works, UH.04, with superheater, at Krimml in July 1929 when almost brand new. It carried the works number 1512/1929. The works numbers at Linz were then in a separate series to those issued from Nunich.

The Engineer

The Pielock superheater. Besides being tried by Gölsdorf it was also applied to a number of locomotives on the Royal Prussian Railways and in the United States. Superheat achieved, on test, ranged from 161°F to 192°F (90°C to 107°C) but the loss of general heating surface tended to offset the gain from the superheat. Moreover the tubes were liable to rapid wear in the superheater where exposed to steam only.

The components of a Brotan boiler

The Engineer

Notes on tables

The following tables are based upon "Locomotives of the Republic of Austria" by permission of J. O. Slezak.

Continental designation of wheel arrangements is used throughout. The following abbreviations are used in indicating type characteristics:

n = saturated steam

h = superheated steam

v = compound

t = tank

Thus a design shewn as 1D h2vt is a 2-8-0 (in Whyte notation) superheated two cylinder compound tank locomotive.

Where classes were created by rebuilding the rebuilding dates are given in brackets.

BBÖ Steam locomotives 1918–38

BBÖ	DRB	ÖBB	Type	Built	Origin	Notes
1	-	-	2B n2	1882–1883	KRB	§
2	-	-	2B n2	1877–1885	KRB GT	Also rebuilt from Class 1)
103	-	-	2B n2	1884–1890	SB	
403	-	-	2B n2	1885	SB	
503	-	-	2B n2	1891–1897	SB	
603	-	-	2B n2	1888–1890	SB	
4	-	-	2B n2	1885–1897	kkStB	
104	-	-	2B n2	1884–1887	KFNB	§
5	-	-	1B1 n2	1883–1884	StEG	§
105	-	-	1B1 n2	1888	StEG	§
6	-	-	2B n2v	1895–1898	kkStB	
106	13.1	-	2B n2v	1898–1902	kkStB	
206	13.1	-	2B n2v	1903–1907	kkStB	
306	13.2	-	2B h2v	1908	kkStB	
7	-	-	1B n2	1879–1880	KEB	
108	-	-	2B1 n4v	1903–1908	SB	
308	14.0	-	2B1 n2	1895–1907	KFNB	
308.500	-	-	2B1 n2	1908	KFNB	
9	-	-	2C n2v	1898–1903	kkStB	
9.400	-	-	2C n2v	1900	SB	
109	-	-	2C n4v	1902–1904	StEG	
209	38.41	38	2C h2	1912–1914	SB	
409	17.6	-	2C h2	(1923–1928)	Rebuilt from Class 9	
10	15.0	15	1C1 h4v	1909–1910	kkStB	
110	35.0	-	1C1 n4v	1905–1907	kkStB	
110.500	35.0	-	1C1 n4v	1906–1909	kkStB	
310	16.0	16	1C2 h4v	1911–1916	kkStB	
12	69.0	69	1A1 n2 t	(1934–1935)	Rebuilt from Class 97	
112	69.0	-	1A1 n2vt	1907	kkStB	
113	33.1	33	2D h2	1923–1928	N	
14	-	-	B3 n2 t	1870	StEG	§
14	98.79	-	B n2 t	1870	SB	
114	12.1	-	1D2 h3	1929	N	
214	12.0	12	1D2 h2	1928–1936	N	
15	-	-	2B n2	1883–1887	ÖNWB	§
116	-	-	2B n2	1860–1864	SB	
116.100	-	-	2B n2	1872–1873	SB	
118	-	-	1B n2	1859–1871	SB	
19	-	-	1B n2	1872	UWB	§

These tables exclude locomotives used on a temporary basis only from November 1918 until mid 1919.
§ Denotes classes allocated to Austria by a decision of the rolling stock commission in 1924.
N = Built new
The building dates are those of the examples used in Austria.

BBÖ	DRB	ÖBB	Type	Built	Origin	Notes
21	-	-	1B n2	1869–1873	KEB	
121	-	-	1B n2	1867–1873	KFNB	
122	-	-	1B n2	1872	KRB	
23	-	-	1B n2	1872–1876	VB	
227	-	-	2C n2	(1913–1916)	Rebuilt from Class 308	
29	75.8	175	1C1 h2vt	1912	kkStB	
229	75.7	75	1C1 n2vt	1904–1918	kkStB	
229.400	75.7	75	1C1 n2vt	(1909–1912))	Rebuilt from kk St. B Class 129	
229.500	75.7	75	1C1 n2vt	1903–1907	SB	
229.800	75.7	75	1C1 n2vt	1909–1920	EWA	
329	35.1	-	1C1 n2v	1908–1909	kkStB	
429	35.3	135	1C1 h2v	1909–1910	kkStB	
429.100	35.3	135	1C1 h2v	1911–1916	kkStB	
429.900	35.2	35	1C1 h2	1913–1918	kkStB	
629	77.2	77	2C1 h2 t	1917–1922	kkStB	629.01-55
629	77.2	77.200	2C1 h2 t	1926–1927	N	629.56-80
629.100	77.2	77	2C1 h2 t	1912–1915	SB	
629.500	77.2	77.200	2C1 h2 t	1927	N	
729	78.6	78	2C2 h2 t	1931–1936	N	
929	-	-	C n2	1868–1869	KRB	§
30	90.10	90	1C1 n2vt	1895–1901	kkStB	
130	-	-	1C1 n2 t	1905–1907	TSB Purchased 1921	
31	-	-	C n2	1877–1880	StEG	
231	34.70	-	C n2	1890–1904	StEG	
32	-	-	C n2	1870–1875	StEG	
34	-	-	C n2	1868–1873	KRB	
35	-	-	C n2	1868–1871	KFJB	
135	-	-	C n2	1871	VB	
46	-	-	C n2	1872–1873	UWB	§
47	53.71	53	C n2	1867–1884	KEB	
48	-	-	C n2	1885–1888	kkStB	
49	-	-	C n2	1860–1869	SB	
149	-	-	C n2	1865–1870	KFNB	
51	-	-	C n2	1871–1888	KFNB	
52	-	-	C n2	1875	Istrianer B.	
52.500	-	-	C n2	1874	SB	
54	-	-	C n2	1872	MSZB	
56	53.71	253	C n2	1888–1895	kkStB	
58	53.71	-	C n2	1884–1897	SB	
59	53.72	353	C n2v	1893–1902	kkStB	

BBÖ	DRB	ÖBB	Type	Built	Origin	Notes
60	54.0	54	1C n2v	1897–1909	kkStB	
60.500	-	-	1C n2v	1905–1908	kkStB	
260	54.1	154	1C n2(v)	1893–1908	KFNB	
360	54.2	254	1C n2	1902	ÖNWB	360.01-02
360.100	54.3	354	1C n2v	1901–1904	ÖNWB	360.11-26
360	54.2	-	1C n2	1906	ÖNWB	
360.500	-	-	1C n2	1906	ÖNWB	
460	54.4	454	1C h2	1906–1909	ÖNWB	
660	-	-	1C n3v	1905	StEG	
61	-	-	C n2 t	1873	KEB §	
62	-	-	C n2 t	1872	KRB Dnj. B	
162	98.12	-	C n2 t	1911–1913	Felixdf-Blumau	
63	-	-	C n2 t	1874	KRB §	
166	-	-	C n2 t	1882–1892	StEG	
69	97.2	97	C1 n2 t	1890–1908	kkStB	Rack
269	97.3	197	F n2 t	1912	kkStB	Rack
(369)	97.4	297	1F1 h2 t	1941–1942	ordered by DRB.	Rack
70	-	-	D n2	1875	KEB	
170	56.31–33	56	1D n2v	1897–1919	kkStB	
170.300	56.33	-	1D n2v	1898–1899	SB	
270	56.34	156	1D h2	1920–1922	N	
470	-	-	1D1 h4v	1914–1918	kkStB	
570	33.0	133	2D h2	1915	SB	
670	39.3	39	1D1 h2	(1926–1929)	Rebuilt from Class 470	
371	-	-	D n2	1853–1854	SB Rebuilt from C2.	
471	-	-	D n2	1871–1872	SB	
571	55.70	-	D n2	1868–1875	StEG	
73	55.57	55	D n2	1885–1909	kkStB GalTr	
174	55.59	155	D n2	1912–1914	kkStB	
174.500	55.59	-	D n2	1910	kkStB	Brotan-boiler
76	-	-	D n2	1884	Arlb (kkStB)	
377	-	-	C n2 t	1899	MAV	
178	92.22	92	D n2vt	1901–1924	kkStB NÖLB FB	
178.800	92.22	92	D n2vt	1898–1920	SchBB/EWA	
178.900	92.22	192	D n2 t	1921	N	
378	93.13-14	93	1D1 h2 t	1927–1931	N	
478	92.25	392	D h2 t	1927	N	
578	92.21	292	D n2 t	1916–1917	kkHB	
79	-	-	D2 n2 t	1885	Arlb (kkStB)	
279	-	-	1D n2vt	1899–1902	TSB Purchased 1921	
379	-	-	1D h2vt	1899	TSB Purchased 1921	

BBÖ	DRB	ÖBB	Type	Built	Origin	Notes
80	57.4	157	E h2v	1909–1920	kkStB	
80.100	57.4	157	E h2v	1911–1915	kkStB	
80.600	57.1	-	E h2	1919	N	
80.800	57.3	57	E h2	(1936–1938)	Rebuilt from h2v	
80.900	57.2-3	57	E h2	1911–1922	kkStB	N
180	57.0	-	E n2v	1900–1908	kkStB	
180.500	57.0	-	E n2v	1907–1909	kkStB	
280	-	-	1E n4v	1906–1907	kkStB	
380.100	58.9	-	1E h4v	1911–1914	kkStB	
480	57.6	257	E h2	1921	SB	
580	58.9	258	1E h2	1912–1922	SB	
680	57.0	-	E h2	(1926)	Rebuilt from Class 180	
81	58.7	58	1E h2	1920–1924	N	
81.400	58.7	58	1E h2	1922–1923	N	
181	58.8	-	1E h2v	1922–1923	N	
82	95.1	95	1E1 h2 t	1922–1924	N	
83	-	-	B n2 t	1884	ÖLEG	
184	88.0	88	B n2 T	1897–1908	NÖLB	
385	-	-	B n2 t	1884–1885	SB	
88	-	-	B n2 t	1882–1883	KEB	
89	-	-	1B n2 t	1892–1899	KTB	
189	88.71	-	1B n2vt	(1903)	Regauged (1106–1435 mm)	
289	-	-	1B n2 t	1851–1852	KFNB	§
91	-	-	C n2	1876	NÖSWB	
92	-	-	C n2	1876–1888	NÖSWB kkStB	
393	-	-	C n2 t	1876–1881	StEG	
94	-	-	C n2 t	1899	BuLB	
394	-	-	C n2 t	1898–1907	SB	
494	-	-	C n2 t	1888	Muhlkreisbahn	
594	-	-	C n2 t	1898	SB	
195	-	-	C n2 t	1879–1882	StEG	
96	98.70	-	C n2 t	1885–1889	Lokalbahnen	
196	-	-	C n2 t	1883	StEG	
97	98.70	89	C n2 t	1878–1906	Lokalbahnen	
99	98.13	91	1C n2vt	1898–1907	kkStB	NÖLB
199	98.13	91.100	1C n2vt	1908–1914	kkStB	NÖLB
399	98.14	191	1C h2 t	1909–1910	NÖLB	
100	-	-	1F h4v	1911	kkStB	
DT1	71.5	3071	1B1 h2 t	1935–1937	N	
DT2	C4idT	3041	B2 h3	1935	EWA	

BBÖ Class	Type		First built	Grate area m²	Heating surface m²	Superheater area m²	Pressure kg/cm²	Cylinder diam	Piston stroke	Driving wheels mm	Weight in working order tonnes	Permitted speed max. km/hr	Axle loading tonnes	Water capacity m³	Coal capacity tonnes
206	2B	n2v	1903	3,0	135	-	13	500/760	680	2100	54	90	14,5	-	-
209	2C	h2	1912	3,6	174	52	12	550	660	1700	67	90	14,3	-	-
409	2C	h2	(1923)	3,1	151	48	14	530	720	1820	69	90	14,3	-	-
10	1C1	h4v	1909	3,7	187	51	15	390/630	720	1780	74	90	14,6	-	-
310	1C2	h4v	1911	4,6	193	43	15	390/660	720	2100	86	100	14,6	-	-
12	1A1	n2	(1934)	1,0	54	-	11	345	480	1410	32	80	13,0	4,0	1,2
113	2D	h2	1923	4,5	198	60	15	560	720	1700	85	90a)	15,0		
114	1D2	h3	1929	4,7	283	78	15	530	720	1900	117	100	17,6	-	-
214	1D2	h2	1928	4,7	283	78	15	650	720	1900	124	100 120b)	17,7		
29	1C1	h2vt	1912	2,0	87	19	14	450/650	720	1574	68	80	14,3	8,3	3,1
229	1C1	n2vt	1903	2,0	96	-	14	420/650	720	1574	67	80	14,0	9,8	3,1
329	1C1	n2v	1907	2,9	152	-	15	450/690	720	1574	60	80	14,3	-	-
429.(100)	1C1	h2v f)	1909	2,9	120	22	15	475/690	720	1574	61	90c)	14,3		
429.900	1C1	h2	1911	2,9	120	22	15	475	720	1574	61	80	14,3	-	-
629	2C1	h2t	1913	2,5	130	29	13	475	720	1574	80	90	14,4	10.5	3,1
629.500	2C1	h2 t d)	1927	2,5	130	29	13	475	720	1574	84	90	15,0	12,0	3,2
729	2C2	h2 t	1931	3,6	171	41	13	500	720	1574	109	105 e)	16,0	16,8	4,4
30	1C1	n2vt	1895	2,3	131	-	13	520/740	632	1258	69	60	14,5		
49	C	n2	1860	1,6	109	-	9	460	632	1245	38	45	12,7		
56	C	n2	1888	1,8	121	-	11	450	632	1258	42	50	14,0		
59	C	n2v	1893	1,8	123	-	12	500/740	632	1258	42	50	14,0		
60	1C	n2v	1895	2,7	131	-	12	520/740	632	1258	54	60	14,1		
260	1C	n2v	1893	2,2	132	-	12	480/740	660	1400	51	60	13,4	-	-
360	1C	n2 n2v	1901	2,7	144	-	13	470/720	632	1364	55	65	14,0	-	-
460	1C	h2	1906	2,7	113	22	12	520	632	1364	55	60	14,0	-	-
170	1D	n2v	1897	3,9	227	-	13	540/800	632	1258	68	60	14,3	-	-
270	1D	h2	1917	3,9	167	38	13	570	632	1258	68	60	14,3	-	-

Footnotes

a) Maximum permitted speed reduced to 85km/h

b) 214 01-07: 100km/h

       08-13: 120km/h

c) Maximum permitted speed reduced to 80km/h.

d) Originally built with Caprotti valve gear but this proved to be of insufficient dimensions and was replaced by the robuster Lentz gear.

e) 729 01-10 only 95km/h.

f) Classes 429 and 80   High pressure cylinder – piston valves
                                  Low pressure cylinder – slide valves

   Classes 429.100 and 80.100   Both cylinders – piston valves

BBÖ Class	Type	First built	Grate area m²	Heating surface m²	Superheater area m²	Pressure kg/cm²	Cylinder diam	Piston stroke	Driving wheels mm	Weight in working order tonnes	Permitted speed max. km/hr	Axle loading tonnes	Water capacity m³	Coal capacity tonnes
570	2D	h2	1915	4,5	198	68	14	610	650	1700	84	85	14,3	-	-
670	1D1	h2	(1926)	4,5	176	49	15	560	680	1574	85	90	14,5	-	-
73	D	n2	1885	2,3	165	-	11	500	570	1100	55	35	13,8	-	-
174	D	n2	1906	2,5	169	-	11	500	570	1100	57	40	14,2	-	-
178	D	n2vt	1898	1,7	91	-	13	420 650	570	1100	49	50	12,4	7,5	1,5
178.900	D	n2t	1921	1,7	91	-	13	420	570	1100	46	50	11,5	5,2	1,5
378	1D1	h2t	1927	2,0	111	24	14	450	570	1100	67	60	11,0	10,0	3,0
478	D	h2t	1927	2,0	110	24	14	530	570	1100	64	40	16,0	10,0	2,5
578	D	n2t	1916	2,0	114	-	13	540	550	1050	58	45	14,5	7,5	2,0
80.(100)	E	h2v f)	1909	3,4	137	34	14	590 850	632	1258		50	13,8	-	-
80.600	E	h2 g)	1919	3,4	142	67	14	590	632	1258	68	50	13,6	–	–
80.900	E	h2	1911		150	27					69		13,8		
180	E	n2v	1900	3,0	184	-	14	560 850	632	1258	69	50	13,8	-	-
380.100	1E	h4v	1911	4,5	176	63	16	390 630	720	1410	81	70	14,0	-	-
480	E	h2	1921	3,8	176	45	14	610	632	1258	72	50	14,4	-	-
580	1E	h2	1912	4,5	192	58	14	610	720	1410	81	70	13,8	-	-
680	E	h2 h)	(1926)	3,4	145	31	14	590	632	1258	67	50	13,4	-	-
81	1E	h2 i)	1920	4,1	190	40	15	590	632	1258	81	55	14,2	-	-
81.400			1922			73					85		14,8		
181	1E	h2v	1922	4,1	190	50	16	620 870	632	1258	81	55	14,0	-	-
82	1E1	h2t	1922	3,4	137	34	14	590	632	1258	95	60	14,4	11,0	3,4
97	C	n2t	1878	1,0	54	-	11	345	480	930	30	45	10,0	4,0	1,2
99	1C	n2vt	1897	1,4	75	-	13	370 570	570	1100	39	60	10,0	4,8	1,2
199	1C	n2vt	1907	1,4	75	-	13	370 570	570	1100	43	60	11,0	6,0	2,0
399	1C	h2t	1909	1,4	54	13	13	390	570	1100	43	60	11,0	5,1	2,0
100	1F	h4v	1911	5,0	224	51	16	450 760	680	1410	96	60	13,7	-	-
DT1	1B1	h2 j)	1935	0,8	42	21	16	290	570	1410	45	100	13,0	6,0	1,8
DT2	B2	h3 k)	1935	Ölf	39	17	18	250	300	910	50	85	12,5	3,4	1,4
Östb 42.27	1E	h2	1945	4,7	200	76	16	630	660	1350	98	80	17,3	-	-

g) 80.600   Small bore superheater
    80.900   Fire tube superheater as also 80.1900, 80.900, 80.3900 (the Dabeg experimental loco.)
    80.4900 (double chimney) and 80.5900 (poppet valves).

h) Lentz poppet valves.
i) 80.10-55   Fire tube superheater
   80.10-55   Fire tube superheater
   81.400   Small bore superheater

j) Luggage railcar
k) Passenger railcar

N.B. The figures for driving wheel diameter show the official dimensions adopted by BBÖ and ÖBB for weight calculation purposes at design stage viz the diameter at half the permitted wear. The diameter when new was 40mm more.
This table is restricted to (i) locomotive types initiated by BBÖ or its shortlived predecessor O. St. B. (ii) such locomotives of the kk St. B and private companies as saw service on the BBÖ.